James Madison University

Harrisonburg, Virginia

Written by Sylva Florence

Edited by Adam Burns, Matt Hamman, Kimberly Moore, and Jon Skindizer

Layout by Alyson Pope

Additional contributions by Omid Gohari, Christina Koshzow, Chris Mason, Joey Rahimi, and Luke Skurman

College Prowler

ISBN # 1-4274-0081-4
ISSN # 1551-1028

Printed in the U.S.A.
www.collegeprowler.com

Last updated 5/15/06

Special Thanks To: Babs Carryer, Andy Hannah, LaunchCyte, Tim O'Brien, Bob Sehlinger, Thomas Emerson, Andrew Skurman, Barbara Skurman, Bert Mann, Dave Lehman, Daniel Fayock, Chris Babyak,The Donald H. Jones Center for Entrepreneurship, Terry Slease, Jerry McGinnis, Bill Ecenberger, Idie McGinty, Kyle Russell, Jacque Zaremba, Larry Winderbaum, Roland Allen, Jon Reider, Team Evankovich, Lauren Varacalli, Abu Noaman, Mark Exler, Daniel Steinmeyer, Jared Cohon, Gabriela Oates, David Koegler, and Glen Meakem.

Bounce-Back Team: Cheryl Lock, Bree Mills, and Amy Patterson.

College Prowler®
5001 Baum Blvd.
Suite 750
Pittsburgh, PA 15213

Phone:1-800-290-2682
Fax: 1-800-772-4972
E-Mail: info@collegeprowler.com
Web Site: www.collegeprowler.com

How this all started...

When I was trying to find the perfect college, I used every resource that was available to me. I went online to visit school websites; I talked with my high school guidance counselor; I read book after book; I hired a private counselor. Sure, this was all very helpful, but nothing really told me what life was like at the schools I cared about. These sources weren't giving me enough information to be totally confident in my decision.

In all my research, there were only two ways to get the information I wanted.

The first was to physically visit the campuses and see if things were really how the brochures described them, but this was quite expensive and not always feasible. The second involved a missing ingredient: the students. Actually talking to a few students at those schools gave me a taste of the information that I needed so badly. The problem was that I wanted more but didn't have access to enough people.

In the end, I weighed my options and decided on a school that felt right and had a great academic reputation, but truth be told, the choice was still very much a crapshoot. I had done as much research as any other student, but was I 100 percent positive that I had picked the school of my dreams?

Absolutely not.

My dream in creating *College Prowler* was to build a resource that people can use with confidence. My own college search experience taught me the importance of gaining true insider insight; that's why the majority of this guide is composed of quotes from actual students. After all, shouldn't you hear about a school from the people who know it best?

I hope you enjoy reading this book as much as I've enjoyed putting it together. Tell me what you think when you get a chance. I'd love to hear your college selection stories.

Luke Skurman
CEO and Co-Founder
lukeskurman@collegeprowler.com

Welcome to College Prowler®

During the writing of College Prowler's guidebooks, we felt it was critical that our content was unbiased and unaffiliated with any college or university. We think it's important that our readers get honest information and a realistic impression of the student opinions on any campus—that's why if any aspect of a particular school is terrible, we (unlike a campus brochure) intend to publish it. While we do keep an eye out for the occasional extremist—the cheerleader or the cynic—we take pride in letting the students tell it like it is. We strive to create a book that's as representative as possible of each particular campus. Our books cover both the good and the bad, and whether the survey responses point to recurring trends or a variation in opinion, these sentiments are directly and proportionally expressed through our guides.

College Prowler guidebooks are in the hands of students throughout the entire process of their creation. Because you can't make student-written guides without the students, we have students at each campus who help write, randomly survey their peers, edit, layout, and perform accuracy checks on every book that we publish. From the very beginning, student writers gather the most up-to-date stats, facts, and inside information on their colleges. They fill each section with student quotes and summarize the findings in editorial reviews. In addition, each school receives a collection of letter grades (A through F) that reflect student opinion and help to represent contentment, prominence, or satisfaction for each of our 20 specific categories. Just as in grade school, the higher the mark the more content, more prominent, or more satisfied the students are with the particular category.

Once a book is written, additional students serve as editors and check for accuracy even more extensively. Our bounce-back team—a group of randomly selected students who have no involvement with the project—are asked to read over the material in order to help ensure that the book accurately expresses every aspect of the university and its students. This same process is applied to the 200-plus schools College Prowler currently covers. Each book is the result of endless student contributions, hundreds of pages of research and writing, and countless hours of hard work. All of this has led to the creation of a student information network that stretches across the nation to every school that we cover. It's no easy accomplishment, but it's the reason that our guides are such a great resource.

When reading our books and looking at our grades, keep in mind that every college is different and that the students who make up each school are not uniform—as a result, it is important to assess schools on a case-by-case basis. Because it's impossible to summarize an entire school with a single number or description, each book provides a dialogue, not a decision, that's made up of 20 different topics and hundreds of student quotes. In the end, we hope that this guide will serve as a valuable tool in your college selection process. Enjoy!

OMID GOHARI ◯ CHRISTINA KOSHZOW ◯ CHRIS MASON ◯ JOEY RAHIMI ◯ LUKE SKURMAN ◯
The College Prowler Team

JAMES MADISON UNIVERSITY

Table of Contents

Introduction from the Author

Three schools in three years—I've got quite the track record. I started on the West Coast my freshman year, the logical choice for a native Westerner, and here I am in Virginia two years later. West Coasters would say, "James Madison, that sounds like a nice school," and although they're right, most don't know any details. Still, they have heard of the name. That counts for something, right? East Coasters know exactly what that "something" is. They know about the national awards JMU has acquired, the breathtaking landscape of the campus, and the admirable surroundings to match. Easterners have heard all about JMU's reputation for academic greatness, and some have witnessed the University's growth from a small, all-women's college, to a blossoming university. JMU's increasingly difficult admissions process is testimony to one thing: a great many people want to be here. You bought the book, so you're at least considering it, right?

At JMU, the grub is decent, the surroundings are breathtaking, the parties are kickin', the teachers are knowledgeable, and the gym is spectacular. However, what it really comes down to is the people. Madison isn't a school that exists solely to crank out tomorrow's elite, like the next Bill Gates or the future president of the United States; however, each year JMU grads step out into the real world, and they are successful. Whatever they put in the shepherd's pie and grilled cheese at D-Hall, it's working. It's hard to convey with numbers and words on a page what makes up a university. Maybe this guidebook's stats will at least begin to pencil in the basics.

Deciding where to go to college is like learning to drive. Learning might involve some arguing with your parents, and steering down windy roads is a given, but once the process is all over, you feel darn good navigating your own course. I'm not here to make that decision for you, or to tell you that JMU will be the catalyst to your success; however, I hope this guidebook will live up to its title, and will at least point you in the right direction. If that direction changes several times, hang in there. If life really is a highway, the trick is finding the right exit to get off. Maybe you will wind up on I-81, taking exit 245 to James Madison University.

Sylva Florence
James Madison University

By the Numbers

General Information

James Madison University
800 S. Main St.
Harrisonburg, VA 22807

Control:
Public

Academic Calendar:
Semester

Religious Affiliation:
None

Founded:
1908

Web Site:
www.jmu.edu

Main Phone:
(540) 568-6211

Admissions Phone:
(540) JMU-JMU1

Student Body

Full-Time Undergraduates:
14,275

Part-Time Undergraduates:
679

Total Male Undergraduates:
5,944

Total Female Undergraduates:
9,010

Admissions

Overall Acceptance Rate:
63%

Early Action Acceptance Rate:
52%

Regular Acceptance Rate:
67%

Total Applicants:
15,013

Total Acceptances:
9,472

Freshman Enrollment:
3,285

Early Decision Available?
No

Early Action Available?
Yes

Early Action One Deadline:
November 1

Early Action One Notification:
January 15

Regular Decision Deadline:
January 15

Regular Decision Notification:
April 1

Must-Reply-By Date:
May 1

Applicants Placed On Waiting List:
1,000

Applicants Accepted from Waiting List:
882

Students Enrolled From Waiting List:
31

Transfer Applications Received:
1,762

Transfer Applications Accepted:
1,029

Transfer Students Enrolled:
607

Transfer Application Acceptance Rate:
58%

Common Application Accepted?
No

Supplemental Forms?
Yes

Admissions E-Mail:
gotojmu@jmu.edu

Admissions Web Site:
www.jmu.edu

SAT I or ACT Required?
Either

SAT I Range (25th–75th Percentile):
1070–1250

➜

SAT I Verbal Range (25th–75th Percentile):
530–620

SAT I Math Range (25th–75th Percentile):
540–630

Retention Rate:
91%

Top 10% of High School Class:
31%

Application Fee:
$40

Financial Information

In-State Tuition:
$5,476

Out-of-State Tuition:
$14,420

Room and Board:
$6,116

Books and Supplies:
$764

Students Who Applied for Financial Aid:
77%

Students Who Received Aid:
48%

Average Need-Based Financial Aid Package (including loans, work-study, and other sources):
$6,342

Financial Aid Forms Deadline:
March 1

Financial Aid Phone:
(540) 568-7820

Financial Aid E-Mail:
loans@jmu.edu
fin_aid@jmu.edu
scholarships@jmu.edu

Financial Aid Web Site:
www.jmu.edu/finaid

Academics

The Lowdown On... Academics

Degrees Awarded:

Certificate

Bachelor

Master

Post-Master Certificate

Doctorate

Most Popular Majors:

21% Business Management, Marketing

13% Social Sciences

8% Health Professions

8% Communication, Journalism

Undergraduate Schools:

College of Arts and Letters

College of Business

College of Education

College of Integrated Science and Technology

College of Science and Mathematics

Full-Time Faculty:

721

Faculty with Terminal Degree:

84%

Student-to-Faculty Ratio:

17:1

Average Course Load:

15 credits (about 5 classes)

Graduation Rates:

Four-Year: 61%

Five-Year: 78%

Six-Year: 80%

Special Degree Options

Combined-degree programs: Physics and Engineering, 3 to 2; Forestry, 3 to 2, non-degree seeking tracks

AP Test Score Requirements

Possible credit for scores 3 to 5

IB Test Score Requirements

Possible credit for scores of 5 to 7

Did You Know?

? James Madison University was originally named **State Normal and Industrial School for Women**. The first male students stepped upon school grounds in 1946 under President Duke.

There is absolutely no excuse for not being involved. JMU has over **250 recognized clubs and organizations**, at least one of which should pique your interest.

Sample Academic Clubs

Getting involved with clubs or activities at JMU is one of the best ways to meet people and to learn about yourself and your school. For example, you could write for JMU's school newspaper, the *Breeze*, sing in an a capella group like the Blues Tones or Low Key, enjoy the outdoors with the Mountain Biking Club, or lend a helping hand with Habitat For Humanity.

Best Places to Study

Taylor Down Under (TDU), Carrier Library, the Loft (on the fourth floor of Warren, often called the Airport Lounge), or the Quad (in sunny weather)

Students Speak Out On...
Academics

"Every teacher I've had here, no matter whether they were exciting or boring, good at teaching, or just good at their subject, seemed to be really interested in the students and the students' well being."

"I find most of my teachers this semester to be more interesting because I'm taking four or five classes for my major. I find that these teachers have so much knowledge, and they are **truly interested in what they teach**, which is definitely motivating."

"**I did not enjoy the general education classes** that I had to take as requirements. I found that they were boring, and the teachers were just as uninterested in them as the students were. However, now that I am in my major classes, I find that I am having more fun. Clearly, it is because I am learning about things that I am interested in, but the teachers seem to be more excited to teach the information, as well."

"**The teachers here are amazing**. They know so much about the subjects that they teach and are willing to help you whenever you need it. Most of the time the classes are interesting, but many times they do lecture on a topic that is not very stimulating."

"For the most part, my teachers have been very good. **They're passionate about their subjects and knowledgeable in their fields**. I'd have to say that all of my classes have been interesting—maybe not every lecture, but overall, they've been good."

"This year, my teachers seem to be really enthusiastic about what they have to say and about the subject they are teaching. They seem to enjoy what they do and **want to get the class involved in class activities**. They are usually upbeat and interesting to talk to; however, there are some teachers that are monotonous and make you feel like you are wasting their time."

"In my experience so far, the teachers have been either very passionate and interesting, or quite boring. Mostly, it's been the former. **The general education classes here are pretty tough**, in comparison to other schools. JMU seems to be really serious about their education system. The key to finding a good teacher, though, is to ask an upperclassman or an older sibling who is good. Some of the best classes I have taken have been ones that other people told me were awesome."

"I'm taking mostly general education classes this semester, and on the whole, these professors could be summarized, in a word, as 'liberal.' **They are very opinionated and vocal about current events** and historical interpretation, and they often add a liberal slant when teaching their course. As far as proficiency, they teach and present the information effectively. This style is new to me, as I'm an ISAT major and my professors in my major more often lean towards an engineering or logical style of thinking; though often they are still liberal, the material is usually presented void of the professors' opinions or beliefs."

"I went to a community college freshman year, and it was pretty fun. However, the atmosphere and the abilities of the teachers were nothing at all like this. Sometimes the professors show videos or make statements in class that make it clear where they stand, but **none of them push their beliefs on you**. On the whole, they are very personable and most are ready and willing to help."

"Classes here are decent, so far. **I really like the religion classes** because they're thought provoking, and I hate the science ones because they seem pointless to me."

The College Prowler Take On…
Academics

At JMU, education is like a piggy bank: you get out of your education what you put into it. Not every class will come as naturally as breathing, and sometimes it takes a little extra "oomph" on the part of the student. On the plus side, the majority of JMU professors really harbor genuine care for their pupils. Most professors are not only knowledgeable in their various subjects, but enthusiastic, as well. It's quite easy to make an appointment with a prof, and the rewards (improved grades, happy parents) are sweet. At JMU, it's not easy to slack off and squeak through with a decent grade. A degree from James Madison University may sparkle and shine someday within a frame on your wall, but be prepared to put in a little elbow grease before graduation day.

Experience is the real meat and potatoes at James Madison. Generous servings of innovative internships, extensive lab work, and research in and out of the classrooms, peer discussions and hands-on homework combine to make a full meal deal. Students can take their pick of 77 different academic programs, which include hospitality tourism management, writing and rhetoric, and women's studies. Interesting programs like these, along with an equally qualified faculty, have helped JMU to gain recognition.

B

The College Prowler® Grade on

Academics: B

A high Academics grade generally indicates that professors are knowledgeable, accessible, and genuinely interested in their students' welfare. Other determining factors include class size, how well professors communicate, and whether or not classes are engaging.

Local Atmosphere

The Lowdown On... Local Atmosphere

Region:
Northern

City, State:
Harrisonburg, VA

Setting:
Small city; rural

Distance from Washington DC:
2 hours

→

Points of Interest:

Blue Ridge Parkway

By the Side of the Road Bed & Breakfast

Campus Art Galleries (JMU)

Civil War Battlefield

D. Ralph Hostetter Museum of Natural History (EMU)

Endless Caverns

Family Drive-In Theater

Fort Harrison

George Washington and Jefferson National Forests

Harrisonburg and Dayton Farmer's Markets

The Joshua Wilton House

M. T. Brackbill Planetarium (EMU)

Massanutten Resort

Natural Chimneys

Reddish Knob

Shenandoah National Park

Stonewall Jackson Inn Bed & Breakfast

Virginia Quilt Museum

Closest Movie Theaters:

Court Square Theatre

40 N Liberty St.
Harrisonburg, VA 22801
(540) 564-1692

Regal Cinemas 14

381 University Blvd.
Harrisonburg, VA 22801
(540) 434-7733

Closest Shopping Mall:

Simon Valley Mall

Major Sports Teams:

Washington Redskins (Football)

Washington Capitols (Hockey)

Washington Wizards (Basketball)

Baltimore Orioles (Baseball)

City Web Sites

www.ci.harrisonburg.va.us

www.hometownusa.com/va/Harrisonburg.html

www.city-data.com/city/Harrisonburg-Virginia.html

www.discoverourtown.com/TownPage.php?Town=273

Did You Know?

5 Fun Facts about Harrisonburg:

- Harrisonburg residents' smiling faces and warm handshakes **match the city's nickname: the Friendly City**.
- Prior to 1916, Harrisonburg's **roads were unpaved** and were only traversed by horses, buggies, and human feet. In those pre-taxi days, two dollars would buy a ride home from a local stable and save you a dusty walk home.
- Don't be surprised if your jaunt around Harrisonburg is accompanied by an odor oddly reminiscent of dog food. Why? **Harrisonburg is famous for its poultry production**. The poultry's feed, a mix of molasses, corn, and other organic materials, produces a dog food smell that is especially strong in wet weather.
- Tourists from China, Japan, and elsewhere have trekked to Harrisonburg to gaze upon one thing—**chestnut trees**. Three of the last, largest chestnut trees in North America are located on JMU's Quad, right outside of Jackson.

Fun Facts about Campus:

- The fountain adorning Newman Lake runs **365 days a year—rain, snow or shine.**
- JMU is **one of the only campuses** in America to boast of having a stream, lake, bridge, tunnel, traffic light, railroad, and an interstate highway running through campus.

Local Slang:

Y'all – Virginia residents' version of "you all " or "you guys."

The Valley – It's really the Shenandoah Valley, but the Shenandoah gets dropped.

The 'Burg – Nickname for the city of Harrisonburg.

Joke on – Another way to say "make fun of."

Soda – Not pop or soda pop in Virginia.

Students Speak Out On...
Local Atmosphere

"As a transfer student, I think Harrisonburg is much more convenient than my last school, and it has basically the essentials of a college town. There are a few other smaller colleges very close to Harrisonburg and other larger ones not too far away."

"Harrisonburg is unlike any other town! It is a small college town with not much in it, considering that **a third of it's population is college students**. However, there are other universities that are very close to JMU: Bridgewater, EMU, and UVA. Because we are in the mountains, there is hiking, and Massanutten is only a 30-minute drive away."

"**The town is full of welcoming people**. Many of them have lived here most of their lives. There's always something to do, and the mountains are close enough to go on hikes. There's one university that I know of, Eastern Mennonite University, just a little ways away. Some good places to visit are Shenandoah National Park, Kline's Ice Cream, Massanutten, Dave's Taverna, and even Luray Caverns."

"Harrisonburg is, I think, a very welcoming place to be. There are many outdoor things to do, as well as indoor activities. Blue Ridge Community College is close by, as well as EMU. There is always something to do on or off campus; **there's no real excuse to be bored here**. I would say things to visit are the local restaurants and the outdoor things such as Reddish Knob Mountain."

"Harrisonburg is going through a huge transition right now from a small town to a larger suburb, so it gives off this vibe that's **a mixture of Southern country life and the more fast-paced suburban lifestyle**. There are a couple other universities present such as EMU and Bridgewater, which are both much smaller than JMU. Downtown Harrisonburg has remained charming despite the city's growth. A lot of the storeowners down there have a small-town mentality that makes them personable and friendly. There are vegetarian restaurants downtown such as 14 Carrots, which I've never been to, but it's supposed to be very good."

"**The atmosphere here is one of a growing town in a rural setting**. The Harrisonburg area is absolutely gorgeous, it is surrounded by mountains and is in this valley that looks like something out of a movie. The locals have Southern accents, mostly, and they are very open to helping out college students. There are other universities nearby: Eastern Mennonite University is across town, and Bridgewater College is just down the road. Bridgewater people come over here quite often because it's so close. If you were going to come here and see something for the day, I would say go to the mountains. Skyline Drive has some amazing trails and views that are more than worth your time."

"Harrisonburg has a very small-town air to it. It's well populated by a college-age cohort; the town itself still holds an agricultural, conservative character. **The closest university would be UVA**. There's a lot to do in the 'Burg, especially in the surrounding mountains and forests."

"The atmosphere here is pretty chill, on campus and off. **Harrisonburg isn't really the most exciting town** to live in, but I wouldn't say there's anything to stay away from either. Eastern Mennonite University is across town; University of Virginia and Bridgewater Community College are pretty close, too."

"If you go to JMU, **you have to take a swim in Newman Lake**. Some girl was supposed to have drowned in there or something, so it's kind of cool in a creepy way to go swimming there. Also, you should check out some of the bike trails and campgrounds around this area. Shenandoah is a really beautiful place, and it would be tragic if you lived here a while without seeing what it has to offer."

"There are townies and some weird people, **but there are also a lot of friendly locals**. EMU is fairly close, but I've never been. There're a few areas of Harrisonburg, which I probably wouldn't want to go in at night by myself, but overall, I'd say it's a pretty nice place to visit and explore. Kline's is great for ice cream; there's even a place where you can paint your own pottery. Coffee shops like the Daily Grind and Artful Dodger are there."

The College Prowler Take On...
Local Atmosphere

If you were looking for a thriving, exciting metropolis, like Miami or New York, you might want to think twice about making JMU your four- or five-year abode. However, if the medium-sized city in the country setting is what gets you going, you should be drawn here like a moth to the flame. Harrisonburg's humble charms are its natural ones: the Shenandoah Valley is a nesting place for magnificent mountains, breathtaking sunsets, and a plethora of outdoorsy activities. While taking a jog around the countryside, you might come across a horse and buggy, or strike up a conversation with a Mennonite.

Harrisonburg may lack huge shopping malls, rambunctious dance clubs, and big city thrills, but the town's historic setting and several local attractions suffice nicely. The 'Burg is growing, with new shopping complexes springing up in recent years. The relative proximity of three other universities (Eastern Mennonite University and Seminary, Bridgewater College, and Blue Ridge Community College) also creates opportunities for interaction and community. And, in the dire circumstance that you crave some sort of megalopolis, Washington DC, Richmond, and Roanoke are a mere two hours down the freeway. All in all, Harrisonburg is a pretty pleasant place.

B-

The College Prowler® Grade on

Local Atmosphere: B-

A high Local Atmosphere grade indicates that the area surrounding campus is safe and scenic. Other factors include nearby attractions, proximity to other schools, and the town's attitude toward students.

Safety & Security

The Lowdown On... Safety & Security

Number of JMU Police:
22 full-time, 45 cadets

JMU Police Phone:
(540) 568-6911

Safety Services:
- Cadet patrols/escorts
- Emergency phones
- Four marked police cars
- JMU safety committee
- Rape Aggression Defense (RAD)
- University safety engineer

→

Health Services:

Allergy shots
Basic medical services
Choices Program
Counseling services
ECPs
HIV testing
Immunizations
Lab tests
Nutritionist
REACH

Health Center Office Hours:

Monday–Friday 8 a.m.–5 p.m., Saturday 8 a.m.–12 p.m., closed Sunday

Open at 9 a.m. on the first and third Thursdays of every month.

Did You Know?

The Silent Witness Form, located online on the Public Safety Web site, allows students to anonymously and confidentially report incidents of crime.

Students Speak Out On... Safety & Security

"Compared with my other college that I attended, this campus is very safe. I wouldn't think twice about walking alone at night."

"I have never felt unsafe while on this campus, be it at two in the afternoon or two in the morning. **There always seem to be police around**; for example, the Harrisonburg PD, JMU officers, or the Campus Cadets."

"Security is tight on campus. I always see at least **two police cars during the day patrolling the campus**, and even more during the weekend. The blue telephones around campus are there in case of any emergencies."

"**I feel very safe on campus**. You can always see a policeman around wherever you go. Campus Cadets are around at night and are more than happy to escort you back to your room."

"I've always felt very safe and secure on campus, even walking around by myself at four in the morning. However, there have been **incidents of stalkers and peeping toms**, which are probably typical, though, of a school with this many girls."

"As a guy, **I feel pretty secure wherever I go**, but I guess as far as cops and stuff on campus, they're pretty cool, and they make my girlfriend feel safe."

"I never lived on campus, but when I am there at night and in the daytime, I feel very secure. There are always police cars patrolling campus, and Cadets patrolling around where the cars can't go. Even off campus, I feel safe. On the weekends when everyone is partying, no one really bothers you if you're walking alone. **They'll just say 'hey' and be on their merry way**. Walking alone down dark alleys or in places that are unlit or deserted is really stupid, and I think that would be dangerous anywhere."

"I feel very safe on campus. **I think it's a very secure community**."

"I have a few friends who are Campus Cadets, and it seems like they are kept pretty busy, always patrolling campus. **There are also always police cars around, on and off campus**. Sometimes, you hear word of a rape or a peeping tom episode, but I guess those happen everywhere, right?"

"Campus itself is very safe. Personally, I've never felt threatened or in danger, but I also try to avoid stupid situations. **Don't be that girl who walks home alone at three in the morning**; it's just not a good idea anywhere."

The College Prowler Take On...
Safety & Security

As with any college, especially one where there are more females, there is bound to be the occasional peeping tom or aggressive, drunk frat boy. However, students pretty much agree when they say they feel snug as bugs in a rug walking around campus, day or night. Campus police make regular visits, visibly patrolling the sidewalks on foot, and patrolling the roads by car. The constant visible presence of the police force, along with the emergency phone boxes, creates a feeling of safety on campus.

Dorm security is taken very seriously at JMU. Doors that access resident living areas are locked 24 hours a day, seven days a week. Public areas are free to all for certain hours on weekdays, but all interior doors to residence areas remain accessible to residents only. In addition, regular inspections occur to ensure complete and effective security exists at all residence halls. Additionally, JMU has placed high-intensity metal halide or sodium vapor lights in areas with heavy student traffic. It goes without saying, however (although I'm going to say it anyway), that common sense is the best precaution. Don't let the relative safety of JMU and Harrisonburg make you feel invincible. Late-night walks by your lonesome through dark alleys, propping open outside doors in dorms at night, and leaving valuable possessions out are not a good idea anywhere. JMU is no exception.

A

The College Prowler® Grade on

Safety & Security: A

A high grade in Safety & Security means that students generally feel safe, campus police are visible, blue-light phones and escort services are readily available, and safety precautions are not overly necessary.

Computers

The Lowdown On... Computers

High-Speed Network?
Yes

Wireless Network?
Yes

Number of Labs:
14

Number of Computers:
370

Operating Systems:
Mac OS, Windows

24-Hour Labs
Hillside Basement PC Lab

Discounted Software

JMU arranges volume discounts and site licenses to reduce the cost of software that must be purchased.

Free Software

Acrobat Reader, AdAware, Linux, Microsoft Office, Macintosh, SAS, SPSS, Spybot, Symantec AntiVirus, Unix, Windows

Charge to Print?

Yes (cost is 5 cents per page)

Did You Know?

If hooking up your computer at the beginning of the year is more stressful than fun, no worries! **JMU offers CMIB (CampusNet Move-In Bonanza)**, a special service available to help students configure their computers to the JMU network, and to answer any questions students might have.

A team of four James Madison University computing students recently won first place in the national Microsoft Windows Challenge competition, which was held this year with the theme "Make the World a Safer Place." The team snatched the $4,000 first place prize with an **airport security checkpoint device** designed to sense and identify potential high-security risks posed by baggage or passengers, according to *www.jmu.edu*.

Students Speak Out On...
Computers

"There are a lot of different computer labs on campus, and you can always find at least one open computer. I think it's nice to have your own computer; it's just more convenient. But if you can't, computer labs would definitely do."

"I have my own computer so **I don't use the computers here very often**. I would recommend having your own for convenience and reliability."

"I have never had the need to use the computer labs because I have a computer in my room. **The network itself is all right**. It has its problems, such as when it crashes and no one can use it. I'm sure that most networks on college campuses have that problem occasionally, and it doesn't happen too often."

"It's helpful to bring your own computer just because it is much more convenient. I haven't had any experience with the computer labs because I have my own computer. If you decide to get a computer, **the laptop is definitely the best way to go**."

"**Computer labs are usually crowded during the day**; however, at night, you can always find one to use. Most people have their own computer with them. I haven't met anyone that didn't have their own. The computer labs are located throughout campus, which helps, too. That way, they aren't all condensed in one area."

"**The only time there seems to be a problem with the network is the first few days of school** when everyone is moving in and setting up their Internet. However, other than that, I rarely have a problem with the network. Computer labs are never crowded; however, sometimes, it's hard to find an open computer in the library. I would advise anyone to bring their own if they could."

"The only beef I have with the campus computer system is this: **there are some people that get on computers just to talk on Instant Messenger** when there are other people waiting to type papers or do some research. There should definitely be some more regulation for that. Otherwise, the computer facilities are decent. You may have to wait a little while for a computer around the middle of the day, especially in the library, but you'll always get a computer."

"Computer technology and availability at JMU is excellent. Especially in the ISAT College, **there are literally computers in every room and on most hallways and study lounges**. Wireless access is available in most of the building, so notepad and laptop accessibility is excellent. Due to the many labs and computer lounges throughout campus, it's not completely necessary to have a personal computer."

"I didn't have a computer my freshman year because I couldn't afford one. So, needless to say, I depended on the campus computers. Most of the time, I did just fine, except for the occasional network mishap, which affects the computers sometimes. Sometimes, **I did have to wait for computers, but not that often**. Now that I have my own computer, though, I like it a lot better. It's a laptop, too, which I think is more convenient."

The College Prowler Take On...
Computers

Most students zip over to a computer to check e-mails, do last-minute research, type papers, or access the Blackboard Web site (the ever-popular place for profs to put course documents, pertinent information, and grades). There is also a notorious crowd who comes in to sign on to AIM and monopolize computers for much longer than the average e-mail or Blackboard checkers. You can try rolling your eyes at them, or making small sighing sounds over their shoulder (many people do!) but most of the time you will get no response. Apparently, IM is just that fun.

The majority of students at JMU toted their personal computers or laptops from home. However, those without shouldn't feel hindered at JMU by their lack of a computer. Labs are easily accessible, large enough to accommodate the general student population, and in various locations throughout campus. Sometimes, you might find yourself eagerly awaiting a computer in one of the busier labs, like the one in Carrier Library. It never fails, however, that within five minutes or so, someone will vacate, and you can go in for the kill. The busiest times in most of the labs are around midday, when everyone is out and about, taking care of business. Rush hour or not, finding a computer to use on campus should rarely be an unpleasant experience.

B+

The College Prowler® Grade on

Computers: B+

A high grade in Computers designates that computer labs are available, the computer network is easily accessible, and the campus' computing technology is up-to-date.

Facilities

The Lowdown On... Facilities

Student Center:

Yes, the University Center, comprised of four buildings: Taylor, Warren, Grafton-Stovall, Phillips Center

Athletic Center:

UREC

Marilyn Crawford Fitness Center in Godwin

The Robert & Frances Plecker Athletic Performance Center

Libraries:

Carrier Library

Various department libraries

Campus Size:

605 acres

Popular Places to Chill:

The Airport Lounge

Barnes & Noble

The Quad (when it's sunny)

Taylor Down Under (TDU)

→

What Is There to Do on Campus?

JMU students have it made. In between classes, you can grab a cup of coffee, research in the library, work out, soak in some sunshine on the Quad, study or check your e-mail at TDU, or play tennis or basketball on any of the courts around the residence halls.

Movie Theater on Campus?

Yes, Grafton-Stovall Theatre behind Taylor and Warren offers late-night showings conveniently located on campus and, on occasion, sneak previews.

Bowling on Campus?

No.

Bar on Campus?

No.

Coffeehouse on Campus?

Yes, TDU, Market One, and the College Center all sport a Java City.

Favorite Things to Do

On a weekend, check out Grafton-Stovall Theatre to find out what's on screen. Regardless, you can watch it for $2.50. Any day of the week, hit up the gym for some racquetball, swimming, weightlifting, running, or kickboxing. Grab a cup of joe at Java City in TDU (a hotspot for students), where you can also kick back and watch local poetry readings and bands or play pool. Students also dig the Airport Lounge on the fourth floor of Warren, take a nap, watch TV, get together and study, watch local bands, choirs, or dance performances, or listen to guest lectures or concerts at Wilson Auditorium or the Convocation Center. Catch a basketball game in the spring or a football game in the fall—just keep in mind that there is more to life than winning.

Students Speak Out On...
Facilities

"The facilities on campus are really great, especially the athletic ones. It seems as though they're always trying to improve and add fields and athletic areas. Even UREC by itself is impressive enough."

"I love the campus facilities. **Some are a little old, but they're still relatively nice**. The new buildings and facilities are amazing, especially UREC and ISAT."

"**JMU is currently renovating many classrooms and buildings and constructing new centers**. I feel that these facilities are very nice and serve their purpose for the students. TDU is a very nice hangout for students in between classes."

"The facilities are awesome! The athletic center is huge and has tons of equipment to use. There are lots of places to eat, and they are really clean. You always have tons of choices for food. The student resource center is also fantastic. You can go there to learn how to do a resumé, look for internships, and even try and figure out what type of career is best suited for you. **The Reading and Writing Resource Center is also great**. There are some really helpful people there who are willing to read your papers and critique them. It is hard to make an appointment sometimes, though, so you have to plan ahead."

"The facilities are very nice on campus. **Student centers are always active as well at the recreation center**. Computer labs are always in use, and the library is, too. There isn't a place you can go on campus and be alone, unless you make a point to be alone and get away."

"The facilities are super nice! **The recreational center is one of the best things about JMU**. The campus also has a lot of areas where students can just chill out or do some homework. Taylor Down Under has to be my favorite spot because it's colorful and comfortable. I go there to do everything from sleeping to eating to cramming for tests."

"The facilities are amazing, the gym (UREC) especially. It is three stories high and has just about everything you could ever want: **swimming, racquetball, basketball courts, fitness classes, and a weight room**. The only bad thing is that it can get really busy because everyone loves it. Elsewhere on campus, all the buildings have been kept up nicely. A lot of them are pretty old because the University is old, but they have character."

"Computer accessibility and networking is excellent. Food is incredible and easily accessible. Also, UREC is an **amazing recreation facility which rivals even the big-business gyms**."

"Facilities here are so cool! I go to the gym and lift weights almost every day, but sometimes, it gets a little too crowded. All the other buildings are pretty nice, too. They're all old, so they kind of seem to fit with each other. And **the Quad is so wonderful**, if only just so we can see chicks sunbathing in bikinis in the spring. I love JMU."

"**I really like the campus because it's really pretty, and it has character**. The Quad is the best when it's hot outside because everyone comes out to be social. We also have a really great library, dining hall, gym, and all sorts of other cool places to go. TDU is really good for commuters and for anyone who needs a quick nap in between classes."

The College Prowler Take On...
Facilities

In the mid '90s, JMU entered a landscaping contest where it placed high among other competitors like the White House and Disney World. It's easy to see why. Elegant, gray stone buildings with white trim dot the main part of campus that is intersected by a railroad and christened with a lake and a fountain, and students at JMU take full advantage of their aesthetically-pleasing surroundings. On one of those same warm, summer days, the Quad will be plastered with readers, sleepers, and Frisbee players.

One glance at the athletic facilities, and you might be confused over whether UREC is indeed a gym or some sort of modern Mayan temple. A tour will prove to you that it is indeed a gym—and a mightily impressive one. With three levels to choose from, dozens of classes to take, multiple courts, indoor or outdoor tracks, a rock wall to climb, a pool, and a weight room, it isn't hard to realize why some JMU students have a veritable love affair with their gym. Although most of the campus consists of the original buildings in their aged beauty, the newer part of campus is splendid, as well, equipped with state-of-the-art computer labs, air-conditioning, beautiful lighting, and expert interior and exterior design. Their only downside is their distance from the main campus.

A

The College Prowler® Grade on

Facilities: A

A high Facilities grade indicates that the campus is aesthetically pleasing and well-maintained; facilities are state-of-the-art, and libraries are exceptional. Other determining factors include the quality of both athletic and student centers and an abundance of things to do on campus.

Campus Dining

The Lowdown On... Campus Dining

Freshman Meal Plan Requirement?

Yes

Meal Plan Average Cost:

$1,054

Places to Grab a Bite with Your Meal Plan:

Chick-fil-A

Food: American

Location: Gibbons Hall

Hours: Monday–Friday 7:30 a.m.–10 a.m., 11 a.m.–9 p.m., Saturday 11 a.m.–9 p.m.

College Store East

Food: Freshens smoothie bar

Location: Lower level of College Center on the CISAT campus

Hours: Sunday 4 p.m.–12 a.m., Monday–Thursday 11 a.m.–12 a.m., Friday 11 a.m.–4 p.m.

The Festival

Food: Entrees

Location: College Center

Hours: Monday–Friday 8:30 a.m.–8 p.m, Saturday–Sunday 11 a.m.–8 p.m.

Festival Java City

Food: Coffee bar

Location: College Center

Hours: Monday–Friday 7:30 a.m.–8 p.m.

Gibbons Hall (D–Hall)

Food: Buffet style with salad bar and deli

Location: Gibbons Hall

Hours: Monday–Friday breakfast 7 a.m.–10 a.m., lunch 11 a.m.–2 p.m., dinner 4:30 p.m.–7:30 p.m.; Saturday brunch 10 a.m.–2 p.m., dinner 4:30 p.m.–7:30 p.m., Sunday brunch 10 a.m.–3 p.m., dinner 4:30 p.m.–7:30 p.m.

Lakeside Express

Food: Á la carte dining

Location: Chandler Hall

Hours: Monday–Thursday 11 a.m.–11 p.m., Friday 11 a.m.–2 p.m., 7 p.m.–1 a.m., Saturday 7 p.m.–1 a.m., Sunday 5 p.m.–11 p.m.

Let's Go

Food: Self–serve deli/salad bar, carry-out only

Location: Gibbons Hall

Hours: Monday–Thursday 10:45 a.m.–3:30 p.m., Friday 10:45 a.m.–2 p.m.

Madison Grill

Food: Dinner foods (e.g., steak, seafood, etc.)

Location: Warren Hall

Hours: Monday–Friday lunch 11 a.m.–2 p.m., dinner 5 p.m.–9 p.m.

Market One

Food: Entrees, coffee

Location: Gibbons Hall

Hours: Monday–Thursday 7:30 a.m.–9 p.m., Friday 7:30 a.m.–2 p.m.

Mister Chips Convenience Store

Food: Campus convenience store

Location: Corner of Bluestone and Dukes Drive

Hours: Monday–Friday 7:30 a.m. –12 a.m., Saturday–Sunday 11 a.m.–11 p.m.

Mrs. Green's

Food: Eat-in or carry-out buffet style with salad bar

Location: Chandler Hall

Hours: Monday–Friday 11 a.m.–2 p.m.

PC Dukes

Food: Entrees

Location: Phillips Center

Hours: Sunday 3:30 p.m.–10 p.m., Monday–Thursday 11 a.m.–10 p.m., Friday–Saturday 11 a.m.–8 p.m.

Taylor Down Under Java City

Food: Coffee bar with some bakery items

Location: Taylor Hall

Hours: Monday–Thursday 7:30 a.m.–9:30 p.m., Friday 7:30 a.m.–6:30 p.m., 11 p.m.–2 a.m., Saturday–Sunday (hours vary according to programming)

UREC Smoothie Bar

Food: Smoothie bar

Location: University Recreation Center

Hours: Monday–Thursday 12 a.m.–9:30 p.m., Friday 12 a.m.–7 p.m.

Off-Campus Places to Use Your Meal Plan:

Pargos Restaurant

(540) 433-5000

1691 East Market St.

Blimpie Subs and Salads

(540) 433-5566

710 Port Republic Rd.

IHOP

(540) 438-9251

109 University Blvd.

Domino's Pizza

(540) 433-3111

41 Burgess Dr.

Subway

(540) 433-9866

2173 South Main St.

24-Hour On-Campus Eating?

No

→

Student Favorites:

D-Hall

The Festival

Mrs. Green's

Let's Go

PC Dukes

Other Options:

The classic brown-bag sack lunch or a quick car ride to Sheetz, located just down the road on University Boulevard.

Did You Know?

Wondering what punches are? While they have nothing to do with fighting, they have a lot to do with eating. Punches are an integral part of every JMU meal plan, big or small. Meal punches are exchanged at many dining locations for entry, and others for pre-ordained meal combinations. Students generally can only use **one or two meal punches** per meal period. You can't use a punch at Lakeside Express, Java City, Mister Chips, College Store East, Smoothie Bar, or Market One at lunch.

To use up extra punches on their meal plans, **students often double punch**, or use both lunch and dinner punches at the same time. Just be aware that you can only double punch Monday through Thursday after 11 a.m. So much for late-night weekend munchies!

Students Speak Out On...
Campus Dining

"Personally, I like the food on campus. There are a ton of different places to eat, and as long as you don't let yourself go to the same place all the time, you won't get sick of what's around."

"The food is always good. I love all the places to eat, especially Festival where **they toast your sandwiches for you**!"

"As far as campus food goes, JMU's is pretty good. There is a wide variety of what to eat on campus, from **Sbarro to Mexican, Italian, delis, and turkey dinners**. D-Hall is always good because it's all-you-can-eat, as is Mrs. Green's, which is a salad bar."

"**The food on campus is amazing**. You have a wide selection of food ranging from the typical pizza to sushi. There are tons of places to satisfy your appetite, and they are located at different places on campus. Some good places to eat are D-Hall (the main dining hall), Let's Go, Mrs. Green's, and Festival. The main dining hall has anything you want, depending on the day you go. They have everything from salad to cheeseburgers."

"The food on campus is not too bad. I've heard from my friends of other colleges that JMU has wonderful food. There's always something you can find that you enjoy and are hungry for. **The good spots are Festival and PC Dukes**. Those are my personal favorites."

"The food is pretty good, overall; although, sometimes, you feel like **you get stuck in a rut of eating pizza or sandwiches** all the time. My favorite places to eat are Sbarro in Market One and Cranberry Farms in Festival, which has Thanksgiving dinner-type foods."

"I love campus food! **D-Hall is great if you want all-you-can-eat**, but it's just typical cafeteria food. My favorite is Festival, because you can't beat Cranberry Farms. At Cranberry Farms, you get rotisserie chicken and a choice of awesome sides like mashed potatoes and gravy, apple cobbler, macaroni and cheese, and cornbread. I also like Let's Go, down on the main part of campus, because it is really good and fast."

"JMU is ranked nationally among public universities in America for great food. **There are numerous locations to eat out**. The best of these is the Festival."

"The food isn't bad for college food. I've heard some real horror stories about college dining, so I consider myself fortunate. **Burgers at Festival aren't bad**, and D-Hall rocks for us hungry guys because we can eat whatever we want, and as much as we want."

"I really like the food around here. You don't really hear too many people complain about it, especially not the off-campus students. **On-campus students complain more**, I guess because they eat it more and can get sick of it. The food here is so much better than at my community college, though, so I can't complain."

The College Prowler Take On...
Campus Dining

A plethora of dining choices are available to students and faculty at JMU, regardless of the size of your appetite. Whether you feel like you could eat a rhino or merely a small salad, you'll be able to find whatever you desire. From do-it-yourself carry-out salad bars to home-cooked turkey and mashed potatoes, it is inevitable that no stomach will leave unfilled. Students agree almost unanimously that JMU's food is wonderful—even amazing.

Unfortunately, as at most other universities, students are grossly over-charged for food. When the cashier rings up your pretzel sandwich at $4.30, you might leave feeling full but ripped off. On the bright side, most dining locations also offer combination meals (in other words, combo meals that only slightly rip you off, not entirely). An example of a combo meal might be a sandwich, chips, and a drink at Dukes. Another benefit of JMU dining service is D-Hall. D-Hall is stuff-your-face eating at its finest. One swipe of your card, and you're admitted into a glutton's paradise. Although you can't take any food out of D-Hall, you probably wouldn't need to if you could. If you're in the mood for take-out, you can do so from just about any other dining location.

B+

The College Prowler® Grade on

Campus Dining: B+

Our grade on Campus Dining addresses the quality of both school-owned dining halls and independent on-campus restaurants as well as the price, availability, and variety of food.

Off-Campus Dining

The Lowdown On... Off-Campus Dining

Restaurant Prowler: Popular Places to Eat!

Applebee's
Food: American
1860 E Market St.
(540) 438-8121
Price: $10–$20
Hours: Daily 11 a.m.–11 p.m.

Bar-B-Q Ranch
Food: American/BBQ
3311 N Valley Pike
(540) 434-3296

(Bar-B-Q Ranch, continued)
Price: $10–$25
Hours: Monday–Thursday 11 a.m.–8 p.m., Friday–Saturday 11 a.m.–10:30 p.m., Sunday 11 a.m.–9 p.m.

Bombay Court Yard
Food: Indian
1588 S Main St.
(540) 442-7166
Price: $5–$15
Hours: Monday–Friday 11:30 a.m.–2 p.m., 5 p.m.–9 p.m., Saturday–Sunday 12 a.m.–2:30 p.m., 5 p.m.–9 p.m.

➜

Boston Beanery Restaurant & Tavern

Food: American

1625 E Market St.

(540) 433-1870

Cool Features: Family and kid friendly

Price: $12–$25

Hours: Monday–Thursday 11 a.m.–11:30 p.m., Friday and Saturday 11 a.m.–1 a.m., Sunday 11 a.m.–11:30 p.m.

Buffalo Wild Wings (BW3's)

Food: American

1007 S Main St.

(540) 438-9790

Cool Features: Wings, beer, and sports—all the essentials

Price: $5–$15

Hours: Monday–Sunday 11 a.m.–12:30 a.m.

Calhoun's Restaurant and Brewing

Food: American, steakhouse

41-A Court Sq.

(540) 434-8777

Cool Features: Free wireless

Price:$15–$25

Hours: Monday–Thursday 11 a.m.–10 p.m., Friday–Saturday 11 a.m.–11 p.m., Sunday 10 a.m.–10 p.m.

Chili's

Food: American

1752 E Market St.

(540) 564-1142

Price: $10–$20

Hours: Monday–Thursday 11 a.m.–11 p.m., Friday–Saturday 11 a.m.–12 a.m., Sunday 11 a.m.–10 p.m.

China Express Restaurant

Food: Chinese

1031 Port Republic Rd.

(540) 568-9899

Price: $8–$25

Hours: Monday–Sunday 11 a.m.–1 a.m.

Cici's Pizza

Food: Pizza

2035-91 E Market St.

(540) 432-9099

Cool Features: Check out the pizza bar for creative pizza combinations! Late-night delivery

Price: $10–$20

Hours: Sunday–Friday 11 a.m.–10 p.m., Saturday 11 a.m.–11 p.m.

Cracker Barrel

Food: American, home-style

121 Pleasant Valley Rd.

(540) 574-3099

Price: $5–$10

Hours: Sunday–Thursday 6 a.m.–10 p.m., Friday–Saturday 6 a.m.–11 p.m.

Dave's Taverna

Food: American

95 S Main St.

(540) 564-1487

Cool Features: Dave's delivers

Price: $5–$12

Hours: Sunday–Saturday 11 a.m.–1 a.m.

El Charro

Food: Mexican

1570 E Market St.

(540) 564-0386

Price: $10–$15

Hours: Monday–Thursday 11 a.m.–10 p.m., Friday–Saturday 11 a.m.–11 p.m., Sunday 12 p.m.–9 p.m.

Evers Family Restaurant

Food: Home-style buffet

6187 S Valley Pke., Mt. Crawford

(540) 433-0993

Price: $7–$15

Hours: Monday–Thursday and Saturday 11 a.m.–8 p.m., Friday 11 a.m.–9 p.m., Sunday 11 a.m.–6 p.m.

Finnigan's Cove Seafood Bar and Grill

Food: Seafood

30 W Water St.

(540) 433-9874

Cool Features: It's the only raw bar in town

Price: $15–$25

Hours: Daily 11 a.m.–2 a.m.

Franco's

Food: Pizza/Italian

225 Burgess Road

(540) 564-0105

Price: $10–$25

Hours: Sunday–Thursday 11 a.m.–10 p.m., Friday and Saturday 11 a.m.–11 p.m.

Hank's Smokehouse

Food: American

49 Bloomer Springs Rd., McGaheysville

(540) 289-7667

Cool Features: Hank's Marketplace, located in the Dayton Farmer's Market, provides hot lunches, deli sandwiches, fresh soups, salads, and take-home meals.

Price: $10–$25

Hours: Daily 11 a.m.–3 p.m., 5 p.m.–9 p.m., deli open 10 a.m.–7 p.m.

Jess' Lunch
Food: American
22 S Main St.
(540) 434-8282
Price: $8–$10
Hours: Monday–Thursday 9 a.m.–10 p.m., Friday–Saturday 9 a.m.–12 p.m., Sunday 9 a.m.–10 p.m.

The Joshua Wilton House
Food: Fine cuisine
412 S Main St.
(540) 434-4464
Price: $25–$30
Cool Features: It's a restored Victorian house
Hours: Tuesday–Saturday 5 p.m.–10 p.m.

Kline's Dairy Bar
Food: Ice cream, coffee
2425 S Main St.
(540) 434-6980
Price: $2–$5
Hours: Monday–Friday 8:30 a.m.–10 p.m., Saturday 11 a.m.–10 p.m., Sunday 12 p.m.–10 p.m.

L'Italia Pizza & Pasta
Food: Italian
1039 Port Republic Rd.
(540) 433-1113
Price: $10–$20
Hours: Monday–Thursday 11 a.m.–10 p.m., Friday–Saturday 11 a.m.–11 p.m., Sunday 11 a.m.–9 p.m.

Little Grill
Food: Healthy, home-cooked food, some vegetarian
621 N Main St.
(540) 433-0961
Price: $15–$20
Hours: Tuesday–Saturday 7 a.m.–9 p.m., Sunday 9 a.m.–2 p.m.

Luigi's Pizza
Food: Pizza
1059 S High St.
(540) 433-0077
Price: $10–$25
Hours: Sunday–Thursday 11 a.m.–10 p.m., Friday–Saturday 11 a.m.–11 p.m.

New China
Food: Chinese
1727 S High St.
(540) 574-0598
Cool Features: Specialties include Szechuan, Hunan, and Cantonese dishes
Price: $5–$10
Hours: Daily 11 a.m.–10 p.m.

Outback Steakhouse
Food: Steak, barbeque
261 University Blvd.
(540) 438-0190
Price: $12–$25
Hours: Monday–Thursday 4 p.m.–10:30 p.m., Friday 4 p.m.–11:30 p.m., Saturday 3 p.m.–11 p.m., Sunday 12 p.m.–9 p.m.

Sam's Hotdogs of Harrisonburg

Food: American

910 Reservoir St.

(540) 433-8727

Price: $8–$15

Hours: Daily 10 a.m.–8 p.m.

Smokin' Pig

Food: American

56 E Wolfe St.

(540) 433-3917

Cool Features: Smokin' Pig covers your catering needs, big or small

Price: $8–$12

Hours: Monday–Saturday 11 a.m–8 p.m.

Thai Cafe

Food: Asian

182 Neff Ave. W4

(540) 433-2201

Price: Appetizers: $2–$5, Entrees: $5–$15

Hours: Tuesday–Saturday 11 a.m.–9 p.m., Sunday 12 p.m.–9 p.m.

Traditions Family Style Dining

Food: Home-style meals

625 Mt. Clinton Pike, Park View Plaza

(540) 438-0301

Price: $10–$25

Hours: Breakfast Monday–Friday 6 a.m.–10 a.m., Saturday 7 a.m.–10 a.m., Lunch Monday–Saturday 11 a.m.–3 p.m., Sunday 11 a.m.–4 p.m., Dinner Thursday 4 p.m.–8 p.m., Friday–Saturday 4 p.m.–9 p.m.

Wood Fired Oven Italian Restaurant

Food: Italian

1550 E Market St.

(540) 438-9663

Cool Features: Reservations only for parties of six or more

Price: $15–$25

Hours: Sunday–Thursday 12 a.m.–10 p.m., Friday–Saturday 12 a.m.–11 p.m.

Best Pizza:
Franco's

Best Breakfast:
Cracker Barrel

Best Chinese:
China Express

Best Wings:
Buffalo Wild Wings

Best Healthy:
Little Grill

Best Place to Take Your Parents:
Joshua Wilton House

Closest Grocery Stores:

Food Lion
1021 Port Republic Rd.
Harrisonburg
(540) 433-4056

Mike's Food Mart
1050 S Main St.
Harrisonburg
(540) 434-7444

Other Places to Check Out:

Daily Grind
Golden Corral
Red Lobster

Did You Know?

Interested in trying some **local home-cooked food**? Stop by Evers Family Restaurant, a Mennonite-run restaurant featuring an entirely homemade menu.

Students Speak Out On...
Off-Campus Dining

"There are a lot of restaurants off campus. There are a lot of the major chains (Applebee's, Chili's, Outback), but there're a few that are local, as well."

"There are tons of places to eat: **small independently-owned restaurants, and chains** such as Chili's and Outback. Those are two of my favorites. I also love El Charro when I want some Mexican food."

"There are the usual chains (Outback, Chili's, Pargo's), but there are some local places that are good, such as **Dave's Taverna and El Charro's**."

"Some of the good spots are Dave's Taverna, L'Italia, and Luigi's. **For dessert, there's Kline's Ice Cream and Bruster's**."

"The restaurants off campus are awesome! We have the usual Outback and Chili's, but **Calhoun's is wonderful**, and many enjoy Dave's Taverna, as well."

"Harrisonburg has a lot of the typical chain restaurants (Applebee's, Chili's, and so forth); however, there are some smaller and cheaper restaurants such as Luigi's, which is a pizza and pasta restaurant that is super cheap. I ate there many times my freshman year, but this year I never eat out. **IHOP has good student discounts**, though, like half-off for students on certain nights."

"I don't get to go to off-campus restaurants very much because I'm poor, but there are some good ones. First of all, there are chains like Applebee's, Red Lobster, Chili's, **Golden Corral, and Outback**. Then, there are some really good restaurants around town that are local and have more of their own style. Some of the ones I have been to and really liked are Dave's Taverna, the Daily Grind, and the Little Grill."

"There are a lot of good restaurants in town, as well as pubs and steakhouses. **BW3's and Calhoun's are among the best around**."

"I don't really eat off campus very much because I don't have enough spending money. **I've heard the Little Grill is really good, though, and Dave's Taverna, too**."

"I am a sucker for the chain restaurants like Applebee's, Chili's, and Outback. Sometimes, you don't really know what you're in for when you try out local places, but I hear that some of them are supposed to be really good. I have gone to Cici's a couple times, and I really liked it because **you can eat a lot of pizza and salad for pretty cheap**. BW3's is really great, too, especially for wings."

The College Prowler Take On...
Off-Campus Dining

The off-campus setting in Harrisonburg gives students a little vacation from the fascinating fresco of on-campus feasting. The 'Burg' has its share of chain restaurants, like Chili's, Outback Steakhouse, Applebee's, and so forth, but many students tend to frequent and praise local dives more often. Students agree that each restaurant has its own charms; for example, wing night at BW3's or grilled sandwiches at the Daily Grind. For those who crave sugar like a hyperactive toddler, Kline's Daily Bar presents a tempting array of ice cream cones and combinations.

On the flip side, off-campus dining can run up your tab and cut down your bank balance. On campus, you need only to walk, and tips are not included—unless, of course, you wish to bravely show your appreciation for the D-Hall meatloaf. Off-campus dining takes more planning than a quick run through the dorm to see who is hungry and doesn't mind walking across the street to PC Dukes. But once you arrive at your off-campus destination, life is a piece of peanut butter pie, whether you dip into a chain like Applebee's or call in for free delivery from China Express.

C

The College Prowler® Grade on

Off-Campus Dining: C

A high Off-Campus Dining grade implies that off-campus restaurants are affordable, accessible, and worth visiting. Other factors include the variety of cuisine and the availability of alternative options (vegetarian, vegan, Kosher, etc.).

Campus Housing

The Lowdown On... Campus Housing

Room Types:

Single: One-person rooms

Doubles: Two-person rooms

Triples: Three-person rooms

Quads: Four-person rooms

Suites: Comprised of two or three doubles or triples; these rooms share a common lounge and sometimes a bathroom

Best Dorms:

Chesapeake

Potomac

McGraw-Long

Bell

Worst Dorms:

Blue Ridge

Eagle Hall

Undergrads Living on Campus:

42%

Number of Dorms:

36

Number of University-Owned Apartments:

1, for grad students only

→

➜

Campus Areas:

JMU's campus is divided into five areas: Skyline, Hillside, Lake, Bluestone, and the Village. Skyline is comprised of Blue Ridge, Potomac, and Chesapeake Halls; Hillside includes Bell, Hillside, and McGraw-Long Halls; Lake is composed of Chandler, Eagle, Shorts, and Tree Houses (Cedar, Dogwood, Elm, Magnolia, Maple, Oak, Poplar, Spruce, and Willow); Bluestone consists of Ashby, Converse, Gifford, Hoffman, Logan, Spotswood, Wayland, and Wampler Halls; and the Village features Chappelear, Dingledine, Frederikson, Garber, Hanson, Huffman, Ikenberry, Weaver, and White.

Bluestone Bits: The Bluestone area houses about 646 upperclassmen and 263 first-year students. Individually, each hall's total capacity ranges from 66–186.

Hillside Hints: About 596 first-year students call Hillside Area home and Bell Hall houses the fewest number of students.

Lake Lowdown: Chandler Hall provides a limited number of singles for upperclassmen. Approximately 280 upperclassmen and 831 first-year students reside in the Lake Area.

Skyline Skinny: Chesapeake and Potomac are the newest housing facilities on campus, and Blue Ridge is fully carpeted. More than 820 students live in Skyline.

Village views: The Village is the place to be—about 1,702 first-year and upperclassmen reside in the area. Some Village rooms are designed for quadruple occupancy, hence the reason there are over a thousand people chillin' here.

Dormitories:

Ashby Hall

Bathrooms: Two rooms share one bath

Coed: Yes

Residents: Freshmen

Room Types: Suites

Special Features: International hall, kitchen facility with microwave oven, laundry, vending services, study lounges, TV lounges

Bell Hall

Bathrooms: Community

Coed: Yes

Residents: Freshmen

Room Types: Doubles

Special Features: TV lounge with adjoining activities room, recreational equipment, kitchens with microwaves, vending services, laundry, part of Bell Hall is a smoke-free community

➜

Blue Ridge Hall

Total Occupancy: 410

Bathrooms: Two rooms share one bath

Coed: Yes

Residents: Upperclassmen

Room Types: Double rooms

Special Features: Full carpeted, vending area, study lounge

Chandler Hall

Total Occupancy: 226

Bathrooms: Shared in a suite

Coed: Yes

Residents: Upperclassmen

Room Types: Suites (two people per room, three rooms in a suite), apartments, and singles for upperclassmen

Special Features: Kitchen, two study lounges, laundry, TV lounge, recreational equipment

Chappelear Hall

Total Occupancy: 198

Bathrooms: Two rooms share one bath

Coed: Yes

Residents: Upperclass

Room Types: Suites

Special Features: TV lounge with vending area, laundry, study lounge, recreational equipment

Chesapeake Hall

Total Occupancy: 410 students

Bathrooms: Two rooms share one bath

Coed: Yes

(Chesapeake Hall, continued)

Residents: Freshmen, Upperclassmen

Room Types: Prime doubles, suites

Special Features: Sand volleyball and basketball courts, study lounge, storage area

Converse Hall

Bathrooms: Two rooms share one bath

Coed: Yes

Residents: Upperclass

Room Types: Suites

Special Features: Tiled or hardwood floors, kitchen, laundry, vending services, study lounges, TV lounges

Dingledine Hall

Total Occupancy: 198

Bathrooms: Two rooms share one bath

Coed: Yes

Residents: Freshmen

Room Types: Suites, quads

Special Features: Kitchen, laundry, study lounge, TV lounge with vending area, recreational equipment

Eagle Hall

Total Occupancy: 434

Bathrooms: Two wings of residents share one bath

Coed: Yes

Residents: Freshmen

Room Types: Doubles, small number of singles

(Eagle Hall, continued)

Special Features: Smoke-free, small kitchen with microwave on each floor, laundry, fully equipped kitchen, TV/study lounge, computer lab and dining facilities in basement

Frederickson Hall

Total Occupancy: 198

Bathrooms: Two rooms share one bath

Coed: Yes

Residents: Upperclass

Room Types: Suites, quads

Special Features: Kitchen, laundry, TV/study lounge with vending area, recreational equipment

Garber Hall

Bathrooms: Two rooms share one bath

Coed: Yes

Residents: Freshmen

Room Types: Suites

Special Features: Kitchen, TV lounge with vending area, laundry, recreational equipment

Gifford Hall

Bathrooms: Two rooms share one bath

Coed: Yes

Residents: Freshmen

Room Types: Suites, triples

Special Features: Kitchen, vending services, study lounges, TV lounges, laundry

Hanson Hall

Total Occupancy: 198

Bathrooms: Two suites share one bath

Coed: Yes

Residents: Freshmen

Room Types: Suites, quads

Special Features: Smoke-free, kitchen, laundry, TV/study lounge with vending area, recreational equipment

Hillside Hall

Bathrooms: Community

Coed: Yes

Residents: Freshmen

Room Types: Doubles

Special Features: Computer lab, two study lounges, laundry, TV lounge with adjoining activities room, recreational equipment, kitchens with microwaves and vending services

Hoffman Hall

Bathrooms: Two rooms share one bath

Coed: Yes

Residents: Upperclass

Room Types: Suites, triples

Special Features: Kitchen facility with microwave oven, vending services, large carpeted study lounges, TV lounges, laundry

Huffman Hall

Total Occupancy: 198

Bathrooms: Two suites share one bath

Coed: Yes

Residents: Upperclass

Room Types: Suites

Special Features: Kitchen, TV lounge with vending area, study lounge, three small laundry rooms

Ikenbery Hall

Total Occupancy: 198

Bathrooms: Two suites share one bath

Coed: Yes

Residents: Freshmen

Room Types: Suites

Special Features: TV lounge with vending area and microwave, kitchen, recreational equipment, study lounge, three small laundry rooms

Logan Hall

Bathrooms: Two rooms share one bath

Coed: Yes

Residents: Upperclass

Room Types: Suites

Special Features: Sophomore Experience hall, kitchen facility with microwave oven, vending services, large carpeted study lounges, TV lounges, laundry

McGraw-Long Hall

Bathrooms: Community

Coed: Yes

Residents: Freshmen

Room Types: Doubles

Special Features: TV/study lounges with adjoining activities room, laundry, recreational equipment, kitchens with microwaves and vending services

Potamac Hall

Total Occupancy: 410

Bathrooms: Two rooms share one bath

Coed: Yes

Residents: Freshmen and upperclassmen

Room Types: Prime double rooms, suites

Special Features: Sand volleyball and basketball courts, study lounge, storage area, kitchen, laundry, recreational equipment

Shorts Hall

Total Occupancy: 208

Bathrooms: Two rooms share one bath

Coed: Yes

Residents: Freshmen

Room Types: Suites

Special Features: Two laundry facilities, study lounge, TV lounge with vending, recreational equipment, substance-free hall

Spotswood Hall

Bathrooms: Two rooms share one bath

Coed: Yes

Residents: Freshmen

Room Types: Suites

Special Features: Kitchen facility with microwave oven, vending services, large carpeted study lounges, TV lounges, laundry

The Tree Houses (Cedar, Dogwood, Elm, Oak, Poplar, Spruce, Willow)

Total Occupancy: 25 per house

Bathrooms: Community

Coed: Yes

Residents: Freshmen, except for Cedar and Elm

Room Types: Doubles

Special Features: Vending services, TV/study lounge, recreation room, kitchen, storage area, laundry, basketball courts and sand volleyball area located outside, Magnolia and Cedar are substance-free halls

Wayland Hall

Bathrooms: Two rooms share one bath

Coed: Yes

Residents: Upperclass

Room Types: Suites

Special Features: Kitchen facility with microwave oven, vending services, study lounges, TV lounges, laundry

Weaver Hall

Total Occupancy: 198

Bathrooms: Two rooms share one bath

Coed: Yes

Residents: Freshmen

Room Types: Suites, quads

Special Features: Smoke-free community, TV lounge with vending area and microwave, kitchen, recreational equipment, study lounge, three small laundry rooms

Wampler Hall

Bathrooms: Two rooms share one bath

Coed: Yes

Residents: Upperclass

Room Types: Suites, triples

Special Features: Kitchen, vending services, large carpeted study lounges, TV lounges, three laundry rooms

White Hall

Total Occupancy: 198

Bathrooms: Two suites share one bath

Coed: Yes

Residents: Freshmen

Room Types: Suites

Special Features: TV lounge with vending area and microwave, kitchen, recreational equipment, study lounge, three laundry rooms

Housing Offered:

Singles: 3%
Doubles: 95%
Triples/Suites: 1%
Apartments: 1%

University-Owned Apartments

The only on-campus apartment building, Dentons, is reserved for grad students.

Bed Type

Bunk beds, some lofts; all beds are twin extra-longs (36 x 80").

Available for Rent

Refrigerators and carpets also available for purchase.

Cleaning Service?

Community baths and lounges are cleaned on a regular basis by residence staff. Residents are responsible for the cleanliness of bathrooms that are not accessible from a common hallway.

What You Get

Single bed with innerspring mattress, individual desk with chair, closet, chest of drawers, ceiling lighting, mini-blinds, telephone, TV cable hookup, Ethernet connection, free local and campus phone calls

Also Available

Hardwood or tile floors, carpeted rooms, air-conditioning, smoke-free housing, themed housing; some suites share lounges with a small sofa, end table, and two chairs

Students Speak Out On... Campus Housing

"Most dorms are nice, but Eagle Hall is a place I'd stay away from. Some people like it, others are too disgusted to step foot in there. Not all dorms have air-conditioning, but it's never been too overwhelmingly hot in the rooms."

"The dorms are dorms. There are a lot of different kinds, from the suites in the Village to just regular halls. Where you want to live really depends on you. **You'll meet more people in a hall dorm than in a suite**, yet a suite gives you extra room and a lot more privacy."

"All of the dorms have their ups and downs. I have lived in the Village for two years, and it's nice because it is so central to everything on campus (the Quad and ISAT). However, it doesn't have air-conditioning. It definitely feels more like a community here. **Logan and Gifford are the nicest dorms** because they've been renovated."

"The dorms are pretty nice, but some of the newer ones are all the way across campus, which is very inconvenient. They have nice accommodations, and most dorms are strategically located **within walking distance to food and other resources**."

"**The newer dorms, Potomac and Chesapeake, are really nice, but they're kind of out of the way**. I'd say the Village is the best place to live because it's dead in the center of campus. But watch out in the dorms without air-conditioning at the beginning and end of the year!"

"I lived in the Village my freshman year, and they were pretty nice. **They didn't have AC**, but they were well furnished and fairly clean."

"There are lots of different styles of dorms. **I lived in the Village, which has suites**. I really liked that because three rooms share a sort of living room that comes furnished, so it was really nice when you had company. However, the Village doesn't have air-conditioning, which sounds more horrible than it really is. Chesapeake and Potomac are the nicest dorms and the newest; however, they're slightly separated from the rest of campus because they're across the freeway. If I could choose a dorm to live in, it would be one of the ones on the Quad; they're gorgeous and conveniently located."

"I never lived on campus because I transferred here this semester. But my friends who live on campus seem to like the dorms a lot. One of the things I think are cool are the suites, because **they each have four rooms that share a living room area**. And they all share a bathroom, which is much better than sharing a bathroom with a whole hall."

"The Village is pretty cool. I lived there freshman year. **I wish I would have gotten to live in one of the new dorms, though**. Air-conditioning would've been sweet."

"I didn't stay in the dorms because I transferred here after freshman year and went straight to an apartment. Lots of people like the dorms, but some people complain that **the ones without air-conditioning are hot**. I don't really know the best dorms, but the newer ones, Potomac and Chesapeake, look really nice. Older places like Garber don't look as nice to me."

The College Prowler Take On...
Campus Housing

An integral part of a typical college student's experience includes living in a residence hall. Students at JMU have plenty to choose from; 35 residence halls house nearly half of the undergraduate student body. The most popular dorms, hands down, are those with air-conditioning, Potamac and Chesapeake. On the other hand, students also rant about the two newbies as they are a bit more than a hop, skip, and a jump away from the main part of campus. Blue Ridge dorm, the farthest away from campus, also receives some dirt from students. Also on students' A-lists are dorms like the newly renovated Logan and Gifford, which are located near the Quad. Other students prefer the Village for its central location and homey feel, although the rooms tend to be smaller in that area.

Dorms give students a place to chill, sleep, and sometimes get busy—with homework, of course. Spotswood, Ashby, Wampler and other dorms in the Bluestone area overlook the spacious, grassy Quad. Dorms like Garber, Huffman, and Fredrickson are less spacious, but offer a sense of community in a central location, and the improved upon Logan and Gifford or brand-spanking-new Potomac and Chesapeake, offer the coveted AC and more modern appeal.

B+

The College Prowler® Grade on
Campus Housing: B+

A high Campus Housing grade indicates that dorms are clean, well-maintained, and spacious. Other determining factors include variety of dorms, proximity to classes, and social atmosphere.

Off-Campus Housing

The Lowdown On... Off-Campus Housing

Undergrads in Off-Campus Housing:
58%

Average Rent for:
1BR Apt.: $250–$550
2BR Apt.: $250–$350

For Assistance Contact:
Off-Campus Life
web.jmu.edu/ocl
(540) 568-6071
herrichl@jmu.edu

Best Time to Look for a Place:
The end of fall semester or beginning of spring semester

Popular Areas:
Ashby Crossing, Campus Condos, the Commons, Foxhills, Hunter's Ridge, Old Mill, Pheasant Run, Southview, Squire Hill, Stonegate, Sunchase

Students Speak Out On...
Off-Campus Housing

"I live in Sunchase, and it's an amazing complex with a pool, tennis courts, really nice clubhouse, and a workout room. Not to mention everyone has his or her own bedroom and bathroom!"

"Housing off campus is definitely a change of pace after freshman year. You go from rolling out of bed and shuffling over to class, to having to find a bus or a parking spot and **having to actually put some effort into waking up in the morning**. But there is plenty of housing to go around, and you can get your pick if you put your name in soon enough. I really enjoy having a kitchen and all of the extra room, but socially, I think it limits you. It's much easier to meet people in dorms than in apartments."

"I enjoyed being on campus my second year because **everything is so convenient here**: food, UREC, and classes. However, I am ready to have my own room and to get away from campus food."

"For the most part, **off-campus housing seems convenient, except for the bus system**, which is inconsistent in picking up passengers from local apartment complexes where many students live."

"**I know there are waiting lists for places off campus**, but I don't known anyone that has no place to live."

"Off-campus housing is excellent, and **there are a lot of good choices**. I have a townhouse off campus, and I love it. It's definitely worth it."

"Off-campus housing is worth it, and it's convenient. Most of the apartments are very close to campus, and there are bus stops everywhere, so **if you don't or can't drive, you don't have to**."

"I love living off campus! There are lots of incidental expenses living off campus that you wouldn't really realize unless you were in an apartment or house. For example: toilet paper, cleaning supplies, Internet connection fees, and electric bills. The only other bad thing about living in apartments is that **sometimes your neighbors can be rather inconsiderate**. Our neighbors above us play music really loud, and run around a lot late at night, so it's hard to get to sleep. Other than stuff like that, off-campus living is the best! It's so nice to have my own space and to be removed from campus a little bit."

"I live in Sunchase now, and I really like it, even though it's kind of expensive. **It's totally cool to be able to throw a decent party once in a while** and have your own bathroom to use. I would definitely recommend staying on campus for at least one year, but then get off. You'll never want to go back to the dorms after you move off campus."

"Off-campus housing is pretty convenient because most of the apartments and houses that you can rent are located close to campus. It sucks living in Ashby because **there's a huge hill to hike up at the end of the day**, but it's good exercise. If you don't have a car, it's kind of hard to get to places like Wal-Mart and the mall. I guess that's what roommates are for!'"

The College Prowler Take On...
Off-Campus Housing

In time, whether it's a week or a year after your freshman term begins, you'll begin to ponder what life is like off campus. Eventually, wearing flip-flops in the shower and walking across campus for breakfast will lose its luster. At that point, students should start perusing their off-campus options, such as a townhouse, apartment, or house. Once students have said "adios" to the on-campus experience, many miss the convenience of being able to roll out of bed and stumble to class without having to sell their souls for a parking spot.

Off-campus housing at James Madison is surprisingly abundant. Dozens of apartments in several complexes are less than a mile from campus. Houses that may accommodate up to ten people are available for rent throughout town. One big bummer is that some of the apartments are located on top of large hills, and the roads are impossible to drive when it's snowing without four-wheel-drive. After taking into consideration everything from bathrooms to parking options, you may feel satisfied enough to pull roomies together and sign a lease. It's definitely worth the cost, although off-campus living demands much extra planning. However, even after considering the cons, students agree that living off campus is a great alternative to the dorms.

B+

The College Prowler® Grade on

Off-Campus Housing: B+

A high grade in Off-Campus Housing indicates that apartments are of high quality, close to campus, affordable, and easy to secure.

Diversity

The Lowdown On... Diversity

Native American:
Less than 1%

Asian American:
5%

African American:
3%

Hispanic:
2%

White:
89%

International:
1%

Out-of-State:
29%

Political Activity

JMU is the 6th most politically active school in the nation, according to *Mother Earth News*. Politically-minded clubs and organizations like Orange Band, the College Democrats, the College Republicans, EARTH, and EQUAL contribute to the atmosphere at JMU. Although the campus is not as ethnically or racially diverse as others in the country, it is diverse in belief and outlook. Madison students are relatively involved in their campus, community, and nation. In general, JMU students do care and notice what's going on in the world around them.

Gay Pride

In general, Madison students are accepting and even supportive of the various sexual orientations present on campus. Clubs like Harmony promote awareness, tolerance, and equality for people of all sexual orientations.

Most Popular Religions

The most prominent religions on campus are Protestantism and Catholicism. Religious houses and organizations, such as the Canterbury Episcopalian house and the Catholic Campus Ministry house, can be found in areas surrounding campus and religious services, and groups meet regularly on campus.

Economic Status

Although JMU students come from various social and economic backgrounds, the majority are from middle-class or upper-middle-class families.

Minority Clubs

Diversity on campus may be low, but JMU seems to embrace the meager amount of diversity that exists on campus. Hundreds of clubs on campus are available for minority students, including but not limited to the Asian Student Union, the Italian Cultural Society, the Middle Eastern Club, Women of Color, and the Latino Student Alliance.

Students Speak Out On...
Diversity

"I don't think the campus is very diverse on a superficial level, but if you look around, you'll find diversity in people from all sorts of backgrounds and life experiences."

"I find that it's pretty diverse, but **most ethnic groups tend to chill together**."

"Unfortunately, the campus is not diverse. Most of the students here come from white, middle-class backgrounds. However, **there are programs in place to diversify the campus**."

"**The campus is extremely diverse**. There are people who are artistic, involved in sorority or fraternity life, and also people who are just here to study and learn more about themselves."

"The campus is very diverse. **I see many people from other cultures** around campus, and everyone is friendly. It's great when everyone interacts."

"This campus is **not diverse at all**."

"Unfortunately, ethnically and racially speaking, the campus isn't too diverse. Most everyone at JMU is **white, middle class, American, and, if they're female, blonde**. The good thing about JMU is that it does embrace the minimal diversity that is around. I am good friends with some people from other backgrounds and races, and I find them to be some of the most amazing people here!"

"Racially, JMU is not very diverse. **It's about as diverse as a diner in the 1920s**."

"Diverse in ethnicity or worldview? **In ethnicity, not much at all; in worldview, it's pretty diverse, I'd say**."

"I have seen and heard of a lot more diversity on other campuses than there is here. It's kind of pathetic, I think. People say that **Admissions is trying to recruit more people of different races** and walks of life, which is good. I hope it works, because I think it's more fun to have people around with different viewpoints. I really miss learning about other cultures from the people who live in them. So hopefully that will change."

The College Prowler Take On...
Diversity

At first glance, JMU may seem to be about as diverse as homogenized milk. On a second glance, you might not notice any more variety until you realize that, at JMU, diversity runs underneath the skin. Taking beliefs, hobbies, and outlooks into consideration, students note that the campus becomes a little less clone-like. Students have commented that minorities tend to stick together, but others stand by the belief that all students at Madison freely and frequently interact. Regardless, many students express woes about the lack of actual diversity on campus, but also realize that the miniscule amount of minorities present should be cultivated.

Recently, the institution has been striving to embrace and encourage diversity on campus by raising awareness through lectures on topics like Islam and globalization, and through events like Women of Color Week. Madison also works each year to recruit larger numbers of international and minority students to the school. However, if you think minorities are lacking, take a gander at the guy-girl ratio at JMU. For the ladies, finding a half-decent fella is like finding a prom date on the evening before the big dance. For guys, it's like being the *Bachelor* every day.

D-

The College Prowler® Grade on

Diversity: D-

A high grade in Diversity indicates that ethnic minorities and international students have a notable presence on campus and that students of different economic backgrounds, religious beliefs, and sexual preferences are well-represented.

Guys & Girls

The Lowdown On... Guys & Girls

Men Undergrads:
39%

Women Undergrads:
61%

Birth Control Available?

Yes. The Health Center provides contraceptives to women students through the Choices program. In addition, condoms are provided free of charge at the Health Center. Contraceptive prices through the Choices plan are as follows: 13 months of OCP birth control and annual exam for $120, annual exam $60, intital Depo Provera Rx injection included in exam and birth control for $120. Additional shots every 12 weeks cost $60 each. Three cycles of Ortho Evra are included in exam, and birth control is $120. Each additional three-month cycle is $60 each, and each addtional 13-pack of pills is $60.

Social Scene

Social is James Madison's middle name (the school, not the dead President). It's impossible not to find yourself at, or at least invited to, a party at JMU on a weekend or weeknight. Meeting and interacting with the opposite sex is never a problem, although the odds of dudes scoring hot girls are significantly larger than the odds of girls scoring hot dudes. On a Friday night, it's definitely easier to locate someone decked out and ready to rumble than someone who's chillin' in his or her pad. Although nearly extinct, rare species of non-partiers do exist, although their habitats have been greatly compromised by settlers of the rather intoxicated sort.

Hookups or Relationships?

The nature of JMU (overpopulation of gals, deficiency of guys) creates a scene that tends to embrace random hookups. Many of the folks who are couples have been couples for a long time, some still sticking it out in relationships that started in high school. Other people (many of the girls) are together with a fellow from a different school; Bridgewater, UVA, and Virginia Tech which are all relatively nearby, making long-distance relationships equally promising. On the whole, however, JMU is like any other school: if you want to hook up, you can make it happen; if not, you can cruise with your ladies or your boys, and window shop without smearing the glass, if you catch my drift.

Did You Know?

Top Places to Find Hotties:

1. UREC (the gym)
2. The Quad on a warm day
3. Parties and frats
4. The tanning salon

Top Places to Hook Up:

1. The Kissing Rock in the middle of the Quad
2. Random parties
3. The football field
4. The stacks in the library

Dress Code

Although JMU kids tend to dress a little on the preppy side—hair tied back with ribbons, decked out in khaki pants and polo shirts with the collars turned up—there is no real dress code on campus. Some students create their own fashion with a wardrobe from vintage and thrift stores, garage sales, and random sale racks. Others go for the baggy pants and skater shoes. Finally, some go for the casual, unshowered look, which is best completed with sweat pants and a T-shirt. The best-dressed award, however, definitely goes to our future CEOs and investment bankers from the CoB (College of Business). You can spot business majors a mile away with their pinstriped pantsuits, nylons, and flawlessly gelled, blowdried, and curled hair.

Students Speak Out On...
Guys & Girls

"There are a lot of guys who are those stereotypical guys you want to avoid, then there are a lot of really great ones, too. The girls are the same way. There are a lot of great people here; sometimes, you just have to weed through a bit."

"**JMU has a reputation for having pretty girls**, especially since there are more girls than guys. There aren't as many guys, but you can find some cuties!"

"The guys are few and far between, but there are some cute ones when you find them! As for girls, most of them would fit **the sorority stereotype of skinny and blonde**. However, there are many different circles here, so if you look, there is something or someone for everyone."

"**The guys are all jerks that just want a piece**, except for a few. Generally, they are good-looking. The girls all seem the same, and the majority are self-centered. There are a few groups of people that are very nice, but they are very hard to find."

"**The guys are few, and the girls are many**! The guys are hot, but mostly, they are already taken. The girls are all hot, but they have to compete with each other, which makes for bad situations sometimes."

"There are a lot more girls than guys, which makes things interesting. **The girls here are generally very pretty**, and I'd say a good 80 percent color their hair. They have a reputation for being blond and slim. The guys are harder to stereotype; there are all kinds."

"There are some really, really hot guys here, but there are also some really hot girls. Unfortunately, there really is a shortage of males around here, which makes life interesting. I have ceased to try and be interested in any guys because I almost always find out a week later that they have girlfriends already. At parties, **it can be kind of intimidating**, too, because the girls are all dolled up and flaunting their stuff to get guys. But guys aren't all that college is about—you just have to keep that in mind."

"There are lots of girls; the ratio is **about 60 percent girls to 40 percent guys**. They are very hot."

"**Guys here are pretty chill**. They like to party, and they love JMU because the ratio here is 60:40. The girls here are mad hot, and there are so many of them. Most of them love to party, too, so that's cool."

"Well, since I'm a girl, I can't really say if the girls are hot or not. There are a lot of really pretty ones, though. A lot of girls look kind of fake, I think, because they are really tan all the time, even in the winter. I think that most of them are really nice, though. And there are some really hot guys around; you just have to look for them. **I have a really great boyfriend** that I've been dating for over a year, so I'm proof of that."

The College Prowler Take On...
Guys & Girls

For the guys at JMU, it takes a glance or two to find some eye candy; for the girls, it may take some serious elbow grease, but they do exist. Although JMU guys are harder to lump into one category, female students lament that all the hot ones are taken. However, not every fella is an absolute cad. At a party, a burly frat boy will slam into you and quickly ask with genuine concern if he spilled beer on you. Try to control your astonished gape, ladies, and accept the unfathomable truth that nice, attractive boys at JMU are not a figment of your imagination. Then tell the poor guy that, although he spilled three-fourths of his Natty Light on your leg, his authentic interest more than covers the party foul. If you're a male reader, do re-read and take note of this frat boy's admirable behavior.

JMU ladies, on the other hand, seem to be largely blonde, tan, and beautiful. These female hordes can be intimidating at times, especially in the party scene. The imbalance of maleness on campus does account for a certain amount of cattiness and competition, both of which alcohol can augment. In addition, JMU girls are famous for looking positively bronze during months when the sun is not shining. However, there are thousands (literally) of down-to-earth, friendly JMU girls out there, as well.

B

The College Prowler® Grade on

Guys: B

A high grade for Guys indicates that the male population on campus is attractive, smart, friendly, and engaging, and that the school has a decent ratio of guys to girls.

A-

The College Prowler® Grade on

Girls: A-

A high grade for Girls not only implies that the women on campus are attractive, smart, friendly, and engaging, but also that there is a fair ratio of girls to guys.

Athletics

The Lowdown On... Athletics

Athletic Division:
NCAA Division I
(Division I-AA for football)

Conference:
Atlantic 10 Conference

School Mascot:
Duke Dog

Males Playing Varsity Sports:
379 (6%)

Females Playing Varsity Sports:
373 (4%)

→

Men's Varsity Sports:

Basketball
Cross-Country
Golf
Gymnastics
Football
Soccer
Swimming & Diving
Tennis
Track & Field
Wrestling

Women's Varsity Sports:

Archery
Basketball
Cross-Country
Fencing
Field Hockey
Golf
Gymnastics
Lacrosse
Soccer
Soccer
Softball
Swimming & Diving
Tennis
Track & Field
Volleyball

Intramurals:

Basketball
Bowling
Flag Football
Floor Hockey
Inner-tube Water Polo
Racquetball
Sand Volleyball
Soccer (Indoor and Outdoor)
Softball
Table Tennis
Team Golf
Ultimate Frisbee
Volleyball

Club Sports:

Baseball
Basketball
Bowling
Caving
Cheerleading (girls only)
Equestrian
Fencing
Field Hockey
Gymnastics
Lacrosse
Outing Club
Roller Hockey
Rugby
Ski Racing
Soccer

(Club Sports, continued)

Softball

Swimming

Table Tennis

Tae Kwon Do

Tennis

Triathalon

Ultimate Frisbee

Volleyball

Water Polo

Athletic Fields

Long Field, Mauck Stadium, soccer and lacrosse fields, JMU Field Hockey and Track & Field Complex

Getting Tickets

Hop over to the Athletic Ticket Office to snag tickets for your favorite JMU sports. The ticket office is located in the D entrance of the JMU Convocation Center and is open Monday through Friday, from 9 a.m. until 5 p.m. Worry, but not too much, about getting tickets for football, men's basketball, women's basketball, baseball, or soccer. Admission to all other home sporting events is free for students.

Most Popular Sports

Hockey, basketball, football (which has drastically improved and is expected to keep the momentum going for the next few years), and IM sports are all popular.

Overlooked Teams

Archery and water polo

Best Place to Take a Walk

The Arboretum

Gyms/Facilities

UREC

As previously mentioned, UREC (University Recreation Center) is new, expansive, and perpetually adored by every JMU student. Fully equipped with everything from cardio equipment to indoor courts, karate classes, and a smoothie bar, UREC is the most impressive athletic facility for miles. It's within walking distance for all on-campus students and many of the apartments off campus, so students have no excuse not to look hotter than hot.

Convocation Center

The Convocation Center (nicknamed the Convo Center) is located just behind UREC, and throughout the year, it hosts intercollegiate basketball games, in addition to concerts, shows, and large meetings. Completed in 1982 and seating 7,612, the JMU Convocation Center was the first to be constructed across Interstate 81 from the original campus.

Bridgeforth Stadium

Bridgeforth Stadium has approximately 12,500 permanent seats and contains an artificially surfaced track and field. Built in 1975 and enlarged in 1981, it also contains racquetball courts and houses the military science department, or Army ROTC. Field hockey, football, men's track and field, and women's track and field play and practice on Bridgeforth's turf.

Sinclair Gymnasium and Savage Natatorium (Godwin Hall)

Godwin Hall was completed in 1972 and named for the governor and his wife, Katherine, a JMU graduate. Godwin Hall contains the Sinclair Gymnasium, the Savage Natatorium, the kinesiology department office, dance offices, intercollegiate athletics offices, and classrooms. The 5,000-seat Sinclair Gymnasium provides facilities for JMU athletes, namely archery, fencing, gymnastics, volleyball, and wrestling. Savage Natatorium houses an Olympic-sized pool with seats for 800 spectators.

Students Speak Out On...
Athletics

"Well, the football team sucks, but they're still fun to watch. Intramurals are huge on campus, as well as clubs. There are tons of teams and sport clubs to get into."

"Varsity sports aren't really that big. The best teams are girl's lacrosse and field hockey, which don't really even yield that big of a crowd. Even though we're not that great, **there's still a relatively good turnout for football**. I think intramurals are really popular. Most JMU students are really into keeping fit and are athletic."

"Unfortunately, the sporting events that most people think to go to are not the ones that JMU excels at. **Our football team is terrible**, and our basketball team isn't that much better. However, our archery team and water polo teams are very good."

"From what I know, **varsity sports have a decent reputation**; however, I don't know that much about intramural sports."

"**There are many varsity sports on campus** and most are pretty good. Our football team could use a lot of work, but others, like women's soccer, are wonderful. Intramural sports are also big on campus, as well as the many club sports JMU offers."

"Varsity sports aren't very big; however, many people participate in IM sports. **JMU has a pretty big IM program**. You can do anything from water polo to ultimate Frisbee."

"I was kind of disappointed when I moved here because the JMU football team really isn't that great. My school freshman year had a decent football team, and **I miss the unity that a winning team can bring to a school**. However, JMU kids still have school spirit without a football team to rally behind. Everybody loves the purple and gold! And there are other varsity teams like field hockey, soccer, and archery that are really good. Intramural sports seem to be almost more popular than the varsity ones. There is a huge variety to choose from for every interest and level."

"Varsity sports are around, but I don't think any of them are exceptionally good or high ranked. However, **there's a lot of school spirit anyway**. Intramural sports are really popular, and they are a lot of fun. Since you can pick coed and the level, you can be as serious or as laid-back as you want with it."

"The stuff that really matters, like football, really sucks here. I sort of wish I would have gone somewhere with a good team, because I really like a good football game. But, I've played some intramural sports, and **they're good for releasing the manly aggression, too**."

"One thing that really sucks here is that our football team is less than great. They really try hard, and once in a while, they'll win, but it's really not very often. The good thing about JMU is that people have tons of school spirit anyway. **Lots of people still show up to watch the games**. And other sports like hockey and basketball are more successful. Intramurals are pretty popular here. I played soccer last year, and I really want to try out more because they are a lot of fun. Intramurals are a good way to make new friends, too; maybe that's why people like them so much."

The College Prowler Take On...
Athletics

JMU athletics isn't known worldwide for its talent and success. However, students agree that they can still have school spirit without a winning team. Homecoming at JMU is a riot, and a source of plenty of purple and gold pride, even if the home football team may score more bruises than points. Older students take a bittersweet trip down memory lane, remembering the days when the football team was worth writing home about. Younger students, however, have developed a grudging fondness for their win-challenged Duke Dogs.

If you really need to root for a team that wins once in a while, follow water polo, archery, or one of the other surprisingly talented but less-mainstream teams at JMU. Or better yet, form your own team. JMU has the facilities, the manpower, and the fan base to create a largely popular and successful intramural infrastructure. So hop on the bandwagon. You could even give your soon-to-be-wildly-successful team a more ferocious name than the Duke Dogs. Maybe something large that clobbers or claws, instead of a small canine that runs around and growls.

B-

The College Prowler® Grade on

Athletics: B-

A high grade in Athletics indicates that students have school spirit, that sports programs are respected, that games are well-attended, and that intramurals are a prominent part of student life.

Nightlife

The Lowdown On... Nightlife

Club and Bar Prowler: Popular Nightlife Spots!

Buffalo Wild Wings (BW3's)

www.buffalowildwings.com

1007 S Main St.

(540) 438-9790

If you love sports, beer, and wings, chances are you'll be a regular at BW3's. The place is dark and smoky, but hey, it is a bar. And you can't beat sports, the tube, and 39-cent wing night every Tuesday.

Calhoun's Restaurant and Brewing

41-A Court Sq.

(540) 434-8777

Calhoun's is Shenandoah Valley's premier microbrewery, featuring 11 original brews with names like "Eat Your Oats Stout," "Honey Blonde Ale," "Calhoun's Kolsch," and "Smokin' Scottish Ale." When the beer munchies hit, Calhoun's also features a menu full of grub that is sure to fill your belly.

The CD Pub

1950 Deyerle Ave.

(540) 432-0610

Every week, the Pub hosts live shows and serves American food and brew continuously.

Casey's

1400 E Market St.

(540) 433-2521

Casey's, located in the Sheraton Four Points Hotel, is the place to be throughout the week. The fun is in the lounge offering DJs, live bands on weekends and Thursdays, and a game night.

Encounters Lounge

VA Route 644

(540) 289-9441

Encounters Lounge at Massanutten Resort serves light meals and, during ski season, cocktails. On Friday and Saturday nights, you can listen to live regional bands, or cut a rug on the dance floor. Just be prepared to fork out a little dough initially, as there is a cover charge.

Highlawn Pavilion

2061 F. Evelyn Bird Ave.

(540)-434-7282

Highlawn is another frequently visited spot in the 'Burg' where the 21-and-over crowd can get their groove on. Open from 10:30 p.m.–1:30 a.m., Highlawn features a full-service bar,

(Highlawn Pavilion, continued)

American food, a dance floor, and live entertainment every Friday by local artists.

The Little Grill

621 N Main St.

(540) 434-3594

Expect cheap drinks and tacky trinkets from other generations, including an old bicycle, a single crutch, and a rusted *Muppet Show* lunch box. And the food's not bad either!

Main Street Bar and Grill

153 S Main St.

(540) 432-9963

Rebuilt after a damaging structure-fire in 2001, Main Street came back strong with dancing, DJs, Ladies' Night, and great drink specials.

Other Places to Check Out:

If you're in the mood for a pre-party road trip, take a ride over to Staunton, only 40 minutes down the freeway. Staunton offers its own nightlife, including bars like Chubby's Sports Bar, Dulaney's Lounge, McCormick's Pub and Restaurant, Mill Street Grill, and Mulligan's Pub and Eatery. Also, catch some jazz at L'Italia on Friday and Saturday nights, or some acoustic local tunes at Luigi's on Tuesday nights.

Bars Close At:

1–2 a.m.

Primary Areas with Nightlife:

Downtown Harrisonburg, apartment complexes, house parties

Cheapest Place to Get a Drink:

The Little Grill on Jamaican theme night (Red Stripe beer for a buck)

Student Favorites:

Buffalo Wild Wings (BW3's)

Calhoun's Restaurant and Brewing

Main Street Bar & Grill

Local Specialties:

Local beer on tap at Calhoun's

Favorite Drinking Games:

Beer Pong

Flip Cup

Beirut

Card Games (A$$hole)

Century Club

Quarters

Power Hour

Kings

Screw the Dealer

Never Have I Ever

Useful Resources for Nightlife:

www.pubcrawler.com

www.beeradvocate.com

www.stiggy.net

Daily News-Record

The Breeze

What to Do if You're Not 21

Apartment and house parties are the in-thing at JMU, and not only for the age-challenged. Foxhills' renowned block parties and Ashby's perpetual weekend soirees are a constant source of entertainment for upperclassmen and underclassmen alike. Since Harrisonburg is no huge city with a raging nightlife, house and apartments are your best bet for an eventful Friday/Saturday night. In all actuality, the parties are so numerous, that they're really all you'll need. Frats are also an option, although they're usually significantly more packed and dirtier than shindigs at non-Greek pads.

Organization Parties

Occasionally, you might get tired of the frat/house/apartment party scene and feel like traversing another route for your weekend entertainment. Check out the JMU Web site (*www.jmu.edu*) and click on one of the calendars to see what's up and coming. Clubs and organizations on campus sometimes put together a dance party or dance lesson instead of recruiting a guest speaker or setting up an informative booth. Some examples of alternative fun are when organizations like the Latino Student Alliance and the JMU Swing Dance Club arrange dances and lessons on weekends. You and your friends can play pool for free almost every weekend late at night at Corner Pocket. With your JAC card and a few dollars, you can settle down for an evening of contemporary or modern dance when the theater and dance department puts on concerts.

Frats

See the Greek section!

Students Speak Out On...
Nightlife

"You can always find a party somewhere at JMU, probably on any day of the week if you know where to look. They're usually a good time, and the people there are usually pretty friendly and willing to share what they have."

"Parties are mostly off campus in the thousands of apartment complexes, and there's usually a lot each weekend. Otherwise, there's **a small bar scene** with places like Alston's."

"Most of the parties are in apartment complexes off campus or in frat houses. There is **only one club in the 'Burg'** (Highlawn), but I am not 21, so I have not been there or to many of the bars in town."

"There **really aren't any parties on campus**, but you can always find a party in some of the local apartment complexes—mainly in Ashby. I have had no experience with the bars or clubs off campus."

"Actually, there are not too many parties on campus, but there are many off in the apartments and frat houses. They are usually crowded, but **a lot of fun and good times**."

"JMU parties bring in a lot of students from other colleges. I always meet kids from other schools that just came for the weekend. **You never have to pay for beer** because people are generally cool with people coming to their parties, even if they don't know you. If you're looking for clubs, this isn't the school to go to. There aren't any."

"There aren't really parties on campus. You have to hike off campus to a house, frat, or an apartment. Hunter's Ridge, Ashby, the Commons, Sunchase, Stonegate, and Foxhills all have some really decent parties on weekends (and sometimes on weeknights!). **People are so nice at JMU**, and it doesn't really matter if you just walk into somewhere that you don't know. Most of the apartments have nasty beer to drink, but some get liquor, which is really fun. I don't really know a whole lot about the bar scene, but I hear that Highlawn is a fun place to go. People go to Chaser's a lot, too."

"If you want to party it up, you've come to the right place. Every night of the week, you can find a place to forget your cares, if you know what I mean. **Some crazy stuff goes down**, but it's all in the name of fun. As for bars, the Pub, Main Street, and Highlawn are pretty good places to go chill and meet people."

"If you want to go to bars and clubs, this isn't really the place for that. Harrisonburg itself doesn't really have much of a nightlife, but the students do. Places like Ashby, Foxhills, and other apartments are always having something going on during the weekends and, sometimes, during the week. **Most of the time, parties get pretty big**, and it's fun to get there and try to guess when the cops will bust the place."

The College Prowler Take On...
Nightlife

House and apartment parties at JMU are where the drama goes down, the beats get dropped, and the hookups are made. The cool thing about Madison parties is that they're hardly ever exclusive; the more the merrier! JMU parties are also a spiffy place to rub elbows with peeps from neighboring schools. Since so many chicks and dudes have significant others from other schools, it isn't uncommon for a Virginia Tech guy and his boys to show up at a party you threw because your friends from UVA were coming up. JMU students like to spice up the mix and attach themes to their shindigs. Favorite party themes that have created some big waves are prom, underwear, pajamas, pimps and hos, waiters and waitresses, '70s, '80s, frat bros and sorority hos, movie stars, and of course, togas.

Creativity and a low budget is the key to having a good time in Harrisonburg, VA. You can't be too picky, because your options are a little slim around the 'Burg,' although there are several bars in town. The older students are the ones most likely to frequent the bar scene, since most are far enough away that they require a set of wheels and a valid ID. Freshmen get a double whammy on this one, being under-age and forbidden to keep a car on campus. If the nightclub scene is what you're thirsting for, I'm afraid Harrisonburg might fail to satisfy. However, Washington DC is only a couple hours away by freeway.

B

The College Prowler® Grade on

Nightlife: B

A high grade in Nightlife indicates that there are many bars and clubs in the area that are easily accessible and affordable. Other determining factors include the number of options for the under-21 crowd and the prevalence of house parties.

Greek Life

The Lowdown On...
Greek Life

Number of Fraternities:
15

Undergrad Men in Fraternities:
18%

Number of Sororities:
8

Undergrad Women in Sororities:
19%

→

Fraternities:
Alpha Chi Rho
Alpha Kappa Lambda
Delta Chi
Kappa Alpha Order
Kappa Delta Rho
Kappa Sigma
Phi Gamma Delta (FIJI)
Pi Kappa Alpha
Pi Kappa Phi
Sigma Chi
Sigma Nu
Sigma Phi Epsilon
Theta Chi
Zeta Beta Tau
Sigma Pi (colony)

Sororities:
Alpha Kappa Alpha
Alpha Sigma Alpha
Alpha Sigma Tau
Delta Delta Delta
Delta Gamma
Sigma Kappa
Sigma Sigma Sigma
Zeta Tau Alpha

Multicultural Colonies:
Hermandad de Sigma Iota Alpha
Los Latinos Unidos

Other Greek Organizations:
Black Greek Caucus
Delta Sigma Rho
Interfraternity Council
Knights of Columbus
Order of Omega
Pan-Hellenic Association
Tau Kappa Alpha

Did You Know?

On-campus sorority and fraternity houses have **a living capacity** of 28 people.

A total of **280 Greek men and women** live in on-campus houses.

Students Speak Out On... Greek Life

"I don't know a lot about Greek life. I do know that you can go through JMU and not be involved in Greek life and still have an amazing time."

"Greek life doesn't take over JMU socially. I think it involves a really low percentage of students. So if you're in it, cool; if not, that's cool, too. **It won't hurt your social life if you're not involved**."

"It's said that Greek life is 18 percent of the campus. However, there are times when it feels more like 50 percent. **I don't feel that it dominates the social scene**, though. There are so many more opportunities for students to get involved in clubs and organizations, and most of the time, you hang out with those people."

"**There is a noticeable interest in sorority and fraternity life** on campus. There are lots of people who are involved, but it doesn't dominate the social scene at all. People accept the fact that there are people in Greek life and those who aren't."

"I'm not Greek, but it does not dominate the whole social structure of JMU. There are many frats or sororities you can be a part of, but **it's not something everyone does. No pressure**!"

"**I haven't gone to a frat party all year**. If you want to be a part of Greek life, be ready to give it a big chunk of your life; it takes a lot of time, energy, and money."

"I'm not in a frat, but **it seems to be a big deal on campus**, and they're very active."

"I don't really know much about the Greek life on campus. Sometimes it seems like there are a lot of Greeks because **you see so many T-shirts with letters** when you walk around campus. It doesn't dominate the scene at all, which is nice. The only frat parties I have been to have been really loud, crowded, and dirty. And they all have steep steps!"

"I'm not really involved in Greek life, except if you count the three sorority chicks I dated last year. **They were all blond and hot**. I don't know what that says about the Greek system, but I had a good experience with it."

"Greek life seems pretty successful here, but it doesn't seem like it's really in your face. You can usually tell who is in a sorority or fraternity by the fact that they are always wearing their T-shirts or sweatshirts. **Frats and sororities will hold lots of charity events** around here, and of course, lots of parties, too. They aren't as dominant here as they are in other schools, though, which I think is a good thing."

The College Prowler Take On...
Greek Life

Greek life at JMU is really only prominent if you make it a big part of your life. Students agree that Greek life doesn't dominate the scene. If fraternities and sororities are your piece of pizza, there's definitely a buffet to choose from. If not, that's cool, too. On weekends, frat houses are great, although crowded. It's certainly the place to be if you're a social butterfly.

Many students don't know much about the Greek scene, but that doesn't mean it doesn't exist. The student body is actually about 6 percent Greek. Of the fifteen fraternities and eight sororities, only ten are located off campus, even though their presence isn't advertised or in your face. Walking around campus, you may notice an abundance of letters displayed proudly on students' chests. Waiting for your friend in the Commons during lunchtime, you may notice booths set up by Greek organizations for charities or social events. Driving down Main Street, you might notice letters on some of the huge, formidable buildings. That is about all the Greekness you will be subjected to, unless you choose to attend a Greek function or become Greek yourself.

B+

The College Prowler® Grade on

Greek Life: B+

A high grade in Greek Life indicates that sororities and fraternities are not only present, but also active on campus. Other determining factors include the variety of houses available and the respect the Greek community receives from the rest of the campus.

Drug Scene

The Lowdown On... Drug Scene

Most Prevalent Drugs on Campus:
Alcohol
Caffeine
Marijuana

Liquor-Related Referrals:
356

Liquor-Related Arrests:
47

Drug-Related Referrals:
31

Drug-Related Arrests:
78

Drug Counseling Programs

Counseling and Student Development Center

www.jmu.edu/cousnelingctr

(540) 568-6552

Services: Substance abuse consultation, education, screening, assessment, referrals, and individual and group counseling

JMU Health Center

www.jmu.edu/healthctr

(540) 568-6177

Services: Alcohol and drug peer-education programs, educational brochures, and health screenings

Harrisonburg-Rockingham Community Services Board

(540) 434-1941

Services: Mental health 24-hour emergency services, intensive outpatient substance abuse treatment, including case management, prevention, consultation, and education services for residents of Harrisonburg or Rockingham County

L.I.F.E. Recovery Program
Rockingham Memorial Hospital

www.rmhonline.com

(540) 564-5629

Services: Intensive outpatient substance-abuse treatment services, including evaluation and assessment for chemical dependency, individual counseling for addiction, ACOA issues, and family counseling

Students Speak Out On...
Drug Scene

"There are drugs, but if you don't want to see them or be around them, then you can make it so you're not."

"I haven't really seen or heard of a lot of hardcore drugs on campus. There is **a relatively large amount of marijuana and drinking**."

"It is present, just like on every other campus. However, **it's not something that you'll see** unless it's something that you are looking for. I have never done drugs, and I have never found that I was in a situation that I didn't want to be in concerning them."

"People smoke pot on occasion, and tons of people smoke. **Alcohol is always abused**, and the majority of the people here definitely take part in it."

"I haven't been involved with any drugs while at JMU, but I know they are present. I haven't heard anything about drugs this year on campus, but **you just know that they're around**."

"A good number of people smoke weed, and there are all different types of people, too. If people are doing it at parties, they're almost always very secretive about it and do it in a bedroom because it's still not universally accepted. **Heavier drugs aren't really talked about**, and I haven't seen a lot of drug activity other than weed."

"I don't know much about it. **I don't see drugs much**."

"Lots and lots of people drink, and lots and lots of people smoke pot. At almost any given party, you can find some room where the door is closed, and four or five people are smoking up behind it, having a good old time. Other than pot and drinking, I don't hear about too many other drugs being used. **The majority of students at JMU are hardcore partiers**, and the minority doesn't drink at all. There isn't really an in-between."

"Drugs? What drugs? Who am I kidding? There are drugs here, and **if you say you don't use them, you're lying**. There's not much hard stuff that I know of, but it does happen. Mostly, pot and alcohol are the things to do at parties."

"I have actually never been drunk before, but I'm almost 21, so I think that will change soon. Most people around here I think aren't like me, though. You can seriously always look just a little and find a party to go to, especially on weekends. When you're walking around campus, **you can hear people talking about their drunken experiences** without even trying to listen. I kind of get tired of hearing it all the time, but it is fun to go to the parties and watch drunk people act stupid."

The College Prowler Take On...
Drug Scene

The drug of choice at JMU is alcohol. Many students don't consider alcohol to be a drug, but they also seem to depend on it as if it were one. Students have taken notice of the large amount of partying that goes on around the Harrisonburg vicinity. They also note that the majority of people at JMU seem to be involved, at some level, in the party scene. JMU's party scene is out in the open, and most people seem to like it that way. However, most people also admit to not feeling horribly pressured to be involved in the scene if it doesn't suit their fancy.

In addition to alcohol, marijuana is used on a regular basis. Often, when walking into a party, faint wisps of pot smoke will waft towards you on a breeze. Following that breeze to its source, you can almost always find a designated room in the house where people are hanging out and toking up. Students are more likely to admit to their weed-smoking habits, to display their pipes, and to want to "share the love" with other party attendees. Hardcore drugs are seldom spoken of, but like any other college community, they are doubtlessly present. At JMU, they are kept very hush-hush.

The College Prowler® Grade on

Drug Scene: B-

A high grade in the Drug Scene indicates that drugs are not a noticeable part of campus life; drug use is not visible, and no pressure to use them seems to exist.

Campus Strictness

The Lowdown On... Campus Strictness

What Are You Most Likely to Get Caught Doing on Campus?

- Parking illegally
- Violating noise codes
- Underage drinking
- Not having a parking pass
- Violating the honor code
- Public drunkenness
- Running stoplights
- Not stopping at crosswalks
- Stealing trays from D-Hall
- Streaking the Quad

Students Speak Out On...
Campus Strictness

"Campus police seem somewhat strict about this stuff, but I haven't really encountered them too much."

"Campus police seem pretty strict. Not having ever lived on campus, I'm not exactly sure, and I have never had a problem living off campus."

"From what I have seen, drinking seems to be something that is more problematic than other drugs. I have seen a good number of people arrested for being drunk in public. However, if people are not stupid and just walking home quietly, then all is well. **The cops aren't out to get people**."

"**Campus police will catch people on occasion**, but that is only if they are in danger of hurting themselves or other people."

"Campus police don't tolerate drugs on campus at all, which I think is wonderful. **JMU's judicial system is one of the best**, in my opinion."

"The first weeks of school they're pretty strict, but then they sort of disappear. I think **on the weekends it just gets too hard to regulate parties** because there's so many, but if you're at a party on a weekday, you have a better chance of getting in trouble."

"I haven't really experienced them much. **They seem fairly slack about drinking**, though."

"Most of the experiences I've had with the police have been when they come break up a party. They really can't do a whole lot because if they busted one person, they'd have to bust the other hundred, so they just make everyone leave. When it comes to writing noise violations, I think they hand those out more regularly. And **when it comes to parking, you'd better watch out**! Campus police hand out parking violations like the world's going to end tomorrow."

"The police are **jerks about writing noise violations**, but they don't really bust anybody except the people who own the apartment or house. When they bust a party, they pretty much just tell everybody to scatter. They won't really bother you, unless you're being a dumb jerk and walking around all loud and drunk. Then, they probably have a reason to arrest you."

"I have been at a few parties that have gotten broken up, but most of them didn't end in any trouble. A couple times, the police will write up a noise violation and kick everyone out. But basically **if you're not causing trouble, they'll just let you walk away**. They probably realize they can't really do much when there are dozens of half-drunk people scurrying around. I think they really do care, though, and if they saw someone being really, really drunk, they would do something."

The College Prowler Take On...
Campus Strictness

Campus police care about the students and the campus, but there's only so much they can do when hundreds of students throw parties every weekend. Most of the time, they just hang around, look tough, and break parties up. Often, they will also dole out noise violations to the hosts. The police intervene the most when a student is making a scene or if they are a danger to themselves or others. Although drugs are not a prominent problem on campus, students also say police crack down on drug violations with extra vigor.

Parties aside, students better beware of parking illegally. The parking police hand out tickets like coupons. Parking illegally can mean anything from staying too long in metered parking, to parking in a fire lane, to putting flashers on in order to run into Festival to grab dinner. The parking police are merciless in their ticketing crusades. They do not care how long it's been since you've had a pretzel sandwich from PC Dukes, or if you are running in to retrieve your umbrella from class on the rainiest day of the year. All they see is flashing lights, and like a cheetah in sight of a gazelle, they close in for the kill.

B

The College Prowler® Grade on

Campus Strictness: B

A high Campus Strictness grade implies an overall lenient atmosphere; police and RAs are fairly tolerant, and the administration's rules are flexible.

Parking

The Lowdown On...
Parking

Approximate Parking Permit Cost:

$152 for a year, $70 for one semester, $1 for day passes

JMU Parking Services:

Parking Deck, MSC 1301
381 Bluestone Dr.
Harrisonburg, VA 22807

(540) 568-3300

E-mail: armentts@jmu.edu

Student Parking Lot?

Plenty, depending on if you are a commuter, resident, or otherwise

Freshmen Allowed to Park?

No

→

Parking Permits

- Faculty and staff get priority on passes and parking spots.
- Commuter passes are easy to come by if you can fork over the cash.
- Freshmen don't get jack because they don't get to have cars.

Common Parking Tickets

$20 - Failing to park in a designated space
$20 - Failing to display permit
$20 - Failing to properly display permit
$25 - Parking in a restricted lot or area
$50 - Parking within 15 feet of a fire hydrant
$50 - Parking in a fire lane
$20 - Parking in a prohibited area
$20 - Parking in a striped zone
$20 - Parking in a CDC/HDC Clinic space
$20 - Parking in a hall director space
$20 - Parking in a housekeeping space
$20 - Parking in a motorcycle space
$20 - Parking in a visitor space
$20 - Blocking another vehicle
$20 - Double Parking
$20 - Parking in a service vehicle space
$20 - Parking on the grass
$20 - Parking in a loading zone
$20 - Parking in a bus zone
$20 - Parking overtime at a meter
$20 - Parking overtime at a timed space
$40 - Parking on the sidewalk
$150 - Parking in a handicap space
$150 - Parking in a handicap discharge area
$150 - Blocking a handicap access area
$100 - Unregistered vehicle
$100 - Displaying an invalid permit
Price Varies - Tow Disconnect Fee

Did You Know?

Best Places to Find a Parking Spot

The Gravel Lot (C1) on Grace Street across from campus has adequate parking, for the most part, and a few potholes to dodge. If you are up for a walk down to the main part of campus, there are lots by Festival (R3, C11) and a couple near ISAT (C10, C12) that are open 24 hours a day for commuters and from 7 a.m. to 7 p.m. for residents. The parking deck is also one of the best places because of its central location, if you can get there early enough to snag a spot (before 10 a.m. or 11 a.m. is your best bet). From 4:30 p.m. to 7:30 a.m., most lots are open to everyone (commuters and residents alike), which means you're going to have to fight the whole world for a spot. On the bright side, the coveted Burrus Lot (B Lot) and Miller Lot (M Lot) open after 8 p.m., providing prime access to Carrier Library, TDU, Dukes, and Grafton-Stovall.

Good Luck Getting a Parking Spot Here!

- The Burruss Lot
- The Miller Lot
- The circular lot behind Wilson Hall
- The fire lane outside Festival

The Clincher

If the end of the semester rolls around and you still have unpaid fines, beware! JMU will place a hold on your record, ruthlessly denying you the right to schedule classes for the following semester or even to graduate without first shelling out the cash.

Students Speak Out On...
Parking

"Parking's no fun. There are just too many kids with cars and not enough places to put them. But if you look hard, you can usually find some sort of parking spot. Whether or not it's near where you need to be, that's a whole different story."

"Parking tickets are given out like crazy. I think **parking is definitely a problem**, and they need to make another parking deck or more space for parking."

"Parking sucks. **There isn't enough parking on campus**. When I do move off campus, I doubt that I'll ever drive my car; I'd rather take the bus, walk, or ride my bike."

"Parking's hard to find during the day, but on the weekends, parking's free and available. **The large parking lots are quite a distance away** from the main academic buildings."

"Parking is a problem. **I haven't had trouble finding a spot**, but they are never close to where you want to park. I know it's hard to just build garages everywhere, but it seems like that would solve some problems."

"**Parking is a pain**, but I heard it's like that everywhere. You figure out how early you have to leave for class to get a spot and you get over it."

"Parking is no fun at all on campus. JMU, like every other school, sells tons more parking passes for cars than they have spots for. **It's all about making money**. So, you just have to allow plenty of time to drive around and hunt down a spot, keeping in mind that when you find one, you will probably be as far away from class as possible."

"The parking situation is horrible. **There are 15,000 students and 900 parking spots**. You do the math."

"**Parking sucks—ask anybody**. I don't even want to get started on that because I'll get too mad."

"Oh gosh, parking is an absolute nightmare. You have to allow so much time before class to find a parking spot and then walk to class. I don't mind if I have someone else with me, but **it's really frustrating sometimes finding a spot** with no one to vent to. Before I figured things out a little better, I was always late to class because I had to park really far away. There needs to be another lot built somewhere or something."

The College Prowler Take On... Parking

Ahh, parking. Previous generations of JMU students doubtlessly lamented about the lack of parking spots, and today's students have gladly picked up their cause. With thousands of cars and less than a thousand parking spaces, students agree it's very difficult finding somewhere to park at JMU. In fact, it's easier to complain about a spot than to actually find one. Since the problem can't be helped, students allow enough time before their classes to battle random traffic lights, score a spot, and hoof it to class.

Whether or not the spot is anywhere close to your destination is an entirely different subject. Since faculty and staff get priority (a.k.a. the convenient, close parking spots), students get the choices of far or farther. It is most likely that when you are late for class you will hit every single red light. It will also probably be windy and raining hard, and the only spot left will be the last corner spot by the little tree in the C4 lot, which, incidentally, is the farthest lot away from anything resembling an academic building. So, if you decide to bring wheels to campus, just be aware that parking is everything but pleasant.

D-

The College Prowler® Grade on

Parking: D-

A high grade in this section indicates that parking is both available and affordable, and that parking enforcement isn't overly severe.

Transportation

The Lowdown On... Transportation

Ways to Get Around Town:

On Campus

ICS (Inter-Campus Shuttle) runs Monday through Friday while JMU is in session from 7:45 a.m. to 7:15 p.m.

Public Transportation

Harrisonburg Transit:
Monday–Thursday
7 a.m.–12 a.m.,
Friday 7 a.m.–3 a.m.,
Saturday 9 a.m.–3 a.m.,
Sunday 11 a.m.–12 a.m.

Taxi Cabs

Cart Transportation Service
(540) 434-8646

Harrisonburg Cab
(540) 434-2515

ABC Cab
(540) 564 - 1241

Yellow Cab
(540) 434 -2515

Fiesta Cab
(540) 438 - 5900

➜

Car Rentals

AES
(540) 434-1541

Avis
local: (800) 230-4898
national: (800) 831-2847
www.avis.com

Continental
local: (540) 433-3549

Enterprise
local: (540) 433-7455
national: (800) 736-8222
www.enterprise.com

Hertz
national: (800) 654-3131
www.hertz.com

Priceless
local: (540) 438-9764

Rent-A-Wreck
local: (540) 438-9761

Steven Toyota
local: (540) 442-1491

Best Ways to Get Around Town

Hoof it.

Snag a Harrisonburg Transit bus (free for students and faculty).

A bike or a moped.

Take your own rig, if you are so fortunate.

Ways to Get-Out of Town:

Airport

Shenandoah Valley Regional Airport, located in Weyers Cave, VA, is the closest airport servicing Harrisonburg. Weyers Cave is approximately 35 minutes from Harrisonburg. Many students prefer to fly from Dulles International Airport in Washington DC, which is 120 miles away.

Airlines Serving the Harrisonburg Area

Delta
national: (800) 221-1212
www.delta.com

US Airways Express
local: (540) 234-9257
national: (800) 428-4322
www.usair.com

Airlines Serving Washington DC

Air Canada
(888) 247-2262
www.aircanada.com

All Nippon Airways (ANA)
(800) 235-9262
www.anaskyweb.com/us/e

American Airlines
(800) 433-7300
www.aa.com

America West Airlines
(800) 2FLY-AWA
www.americawest.com

(Airlines Servicing Washington DC, continued)

Austrian Airlines
(800) 843-0002
www.aua.com

British Airways
(800) 247-9297
www.britishairways.com

Continental
(800) 525-0280
www.continental.com

Delta
(800) 221-1212
www.delta.com

Frontier
(800) 265-5505
www.frontierairlines.com

JetBlue
(800) 538-2583
www.jetblue.com

Northwest Airlines
(800) 225-2525

Song
(800) 359-7664)
www.flysong.com

Grupo Taca
(800) 535-8780
www.taca.com

Ted
(800) 225-5833
www.flyted.com

United Airlines
(800) 241-6522

US Airways
(800) 428-4322
www.usairways.com

Virgin
(800) 862-8621
www.virgin.com

How to Get to the Airport

Shenandoah Valley Regional Airport Shuttle (*www.flyshd.com*) leaves the JMU Visitor Center on campus approximately once every hour.

A Goff Buscom
(540) 434-0900

A cab ride to the airport costs around $40, one way.

Greyhound

Greyhound offers three trips daily to Harrisonburg, leaving Dulles International Airport's main terminal from Curb 1D at 11 a.m., 2 p.m., and 7:10 p.m. You can purchase your ticket for $28 upon boarding the bus. The Greyhound station is located about four miles from the JMU campus.

Greyhound Bus Lines
3355 S Main St.
Harrisonburg, VA 22801-2679
local: (540) 434-8052
national: (800) 231-2222
www.greyhound.com

Homerides

A bus that provides students from JMU and other schools in VA rides to certain areas around the state.

→

Amtrak

The closest Amtrak is located in Staunton, VA, approximately 30 miles south of Harrisonburg.

national: (800) 872-7245
www.amtrak.com

Travel Agents

Carlson Wagonlit Travel
39 Burgess Rd.
Harrisonburg, VA 22801-9731
(540) 949-4545

Harrisonburg Travel Center
3355 S Main St.
Harrisonburg, VA 22801-2679
(540) 434-0805

(Travel Agents, continued

Travel Counsellors Inc
435 S Main St.
Harrisonburg, VA 22801-3608
(540) 434-2843

Turner Travel Service
614 Hawkins St.
Harrisonburg, VA 22801-4312
(540) 433-2438

Students Speak Out On...
Transportation

"The bus system in Harrisonburg is really convenient. Even though sometimes it seems like a hassle, in the long run trying to get from place to place is pretty easy. A lot of times it's easier than trying to find parking somewhere."

"I take the bus everyday, and **I think they do a good job** covering all the areas on and off campus. I'm pleased with it."

"The bus system, for the most part, is reliable. **There are buses running constantly**; they run more to the apartment complexes than around town, but they are available."

"The bus system is not that convenient and is often unreliable. **It's definitely better to have your own car**."

"**Buses are free and run very often**. The drivers are quite nice, and the system is easy to learn."

"The bus system is **very convenient** as long as you get pick-up and drop-off times right."

"The Harrisonburg bus system is pretty decent. They would run a little early or late at the beginning of the year, but they're pretty much punctual now. **All the bus drivers are very friendly** and will go out of their way, if they can, to help you make a connection. Sometimes, the buses get pretty crowded, but it's really not a bad system."

"The public bus system is awesome, although not always on time. **You can get around town easily without a car**."

"For a while, I didn't have a car so I rode the bus a lot. Sometimes you have to wait around for the bus to come. **It sucks in cold or rainy weather**, but if you have an umbrella and a good book, it's not so bad. The bus drivers are really nice, too, and fun to talk to if you have an extra minute. At night, they are great, too, for getting from one party to another."

The College Prowler Take On... Transportation

Although a considerable amount of students, especially upperclassmen, utilize their own rigs for transportation, many others dig public transportation. The buses run every half-hour, give or take a few minutes, which is fairly convenient. Students agree that once you've mastered the schedule, taking the bus isn't too much of a chore. The busiest times to ride seem to be mid- to late-afternoon and evening, when the entire non-morning crowd is finishing up classes and heading home. Most students agree that cramped conditions are still manageable in light of the fact that they won't have to fight tooth and nail for a parking spot or spend time walking home.

While the most packed moments come later in the day, the most entertaining ones come late at night. The first night bus circles town around 7 p.m., and the last leaves at 3 a.m. The eight hours in between are a riot. The 'Burg's transit system becomes something of a drunk bus for party animals who are slightly tipsy to hopelessly inebriated and everywhere in between. Fortunately, the bus drivers are incredibly nice individuals, day or night. So, even in your woozy state, remember to say thank you upon exiting, even if it sounds more like "tango."

B-

The College Prowler® Grade on

Transportation: B-

A high grade for Transportation indicates that campus buses, public buses, cabs, and rental cars are readily-available and affordable. Other determining factors include proximity to an airport and the necessity of transportation.

Weather

The Lowdown On... Weather

Average Temperature:

Fall:	62 °F
Winter:	33 °F
Spring:	56 °F
Summer:	77 °F

Average Precipitation:

Fall:	3.02 in.
Winter:	3.38 in.
Spring:	3.15 in.
Summer:	2.37 in.

Students Speak Out On... Weather

"The weather is very unpredictable because we're in a valley, or at least I think this is why we get a lot of wind. I often wonder why I do my hair. Bring clothing for every type of weather condition."

"The weather is beautiful. **There's a definite winter**, but it's mild, and it gets warm pretty quick."

"There are **hot summers and cold winters** along with windy, early springs."

"Definitely bring warm clothes for the chilly winter months. In general, **bring layered clothing** because temperatures change from building to building, and from season to season. Definitely bring comfortable walking shoes! There are lots of hills to walk up and down. The winters can be freezing, but in general, it's warm even in the fall."

"**We get every season**, so bring a good range of clothing. We get snow, ice, hail, and rain—everything from sunny days to code-red days."

"The weather's unpredictable, but that's the East Coast for you. The winters get really cold, and the summers are warm. There's always those days in the middle that throw you off, like those 60 degree days in February and those chilly days in May. My advice? **Wear layers**."

"When it's sunny here, Harrisonburg is the most amazing place to be. **The sunshine brings out the best in the city**. Sometimes, we get some interesting weather, too, like floods, hurricane warnings, big thunderstorms, and snow storms."

"You get all the seasons. It's pretty cold in the winter, there's plenty of snow, and it's pretty warm in the summer. **The wind is usually blowing**, and there's plenty of rain."

"The weather here is crazy! **It's winter one day, and summer a couple days later**. You have to be prepared for it. I have learned to always keep a sweatshirt, a beanie, and an extra coat in the bottom drawer, because I usually have to pull them out."

"Make sure you bring an umbrella! It rains quite a bit here, especially in the springtime. And it's not always warm rain, so **make sure you have good shoes and a warm coat**. Bring lots of tank tops and stuff, too, because it can get really warm. I guess the best I could say is just to have a lot of different clothes for any kind of weather."

The College Prowler Take On...
Weather

After a month or two in Harrisonburg, students have experienced a spectrum of weather, from the chilly to the muggy. Although Harrisonburg does receive all four seasons, students agree that the key to beating the random array of weather in the 'Burg is variety. The Shenandoah Valley is one place where you can get away with having a drawer full of both sweaters and tank tops at any time of year. In addition, students advise you wear lots of layers. Also, the wind around town is nothing less than obnoxiously gusty, so bring a good windbreaker with a drawstring hood.

At JMU, the weather is extremely unreliable. To be prepared, pack like you're going on vacation and you don't know which country you'll end up in. For those sporadic summery spells in the midst of winter, have a couple of tank tops or a pair of cargo shorts. For those artic blasts that may occur between spring rains and blooming flowers, keep a couple sweaters, a hat, and some gloves close by. Keep in mind that it's not unlikely in Harrisonburg to see temperatures ranging from the 20s to the 70s in the same seven days. Another important note: if *Weather.com* predicts a 10 percent chance of rain or more, bring your umbrella. The percentage doesn't mean anything; it just means rain.

B

The College Prowler® Grade on

Weather: B

A high Weather grade designates that temperatures are mild and rarely reach extremes, that the campus tends to be sunny rather than rainy, and that weather is fairly consistent rather than unpredictable.

JAMES MADISON UNIVERSITY

Report Card Summary

Grade	Category	Grade	Category
B	ACADEMICS	B	GUYS
B-	LOCAL ATMOSPHERE	A-	GIRLS
A	SAFETY & SECURITY	B-	ATHLETICS
B+	COMPUTERS	B	NIGHTLIFE
A	FACILITIES	B+	GREEK LIFE
B+	CAMPUS DINING	B-	DRUG SCENE
C	OFF-CAMPUS DINING	B	CAMPUS STRICTNESS
B+	CAMPUS HOUSING	D-	PARKING
B+	OFF-CAMPUS HOUSING	B-	TRANSPORTATION
D-	DIVERSITY	B	WEATHER

Overall Experience

Students Speak Out On... Overall Experience

"Overall, I've had a great experience here at JMU. It's something so different than I've ever experienced. The people here are so friendly, and they want to make sure that you have a good time and enjoy yourself."

"Being a transfer student, I couldn't be more pleased. I wish there was more of a bar scene, but other than that, **everything around here runs really smoothly**. The people are so friendly (staff and students), and you can feel welcome anywhere. Not to mention the beautiful campus buildings and landscape!"

"I can't see myself anywhere else but here at JMU. **The atmosphere here is friendly and fun**, but people are also here to get an education. I feel like it's a good mix; not too big or too small, but just right!"

"The faculty is really here to help you learn, and they care more about an individual's learning experience than most colleges, I think. They dedicate themselves to each and every person. Overall, it's okay. **The social scene is definitely not for people who don't drink** or don't like parties. I do wish I had chosen another college because the majority of the people I have met care only about getting drunk and partying, rather than their education."

"I love it here! I wouldn't even think about transferring anywhere else. The people are all amazing, and **I have made some amazing friends**. The atmosphere is always welcoming, and I feel at home here."

"I love JMU, and I've learned a lot since I've been at college. Sometimes, I've wondered if I'd be happier at a bigger school where sports were more important and the school was better known, but I can't imagine feeling more at ease than I do here. **The campus is beautiful, the people are nice, the teachers are great**, and I really can't complain."

"**I feel like I have finally found a place where I belong**. JMU is home to me. The people are absolutely amazing, and most of the teachers are wonderful individuals with an incredible amount of knowledge to share. I love the outdoorsy environment, and the view of the mountains absolutely makes me smile every time. I am so excited to come back next year, and this year isn't even over yet! This is a truly unique school, filled with a healthy and contagious energy."

"I love JMU. **It's a great place to study** and to live. I wouldn't want to be anywhere else."

"JMU is such a cool place to go to school. **I think the teachers really are pretty good on the whole**, and the people are so fun. The girls are so hot, too. There is a lot to do around here, if you are into being outdoors or into traveling a little to go to DC or Charlottesville or somewhere. I am very glad I that chose this school. I have no regrets."

"I thought about going to other colleges instead of this one, but I am really happy with the choice I made. Since I'm from Northern Virginia, it makes sense for me to be pretty close to home, and to be able to drive up for the weekend if I want to. The drive is really pretty, too, because, of course, this area is really pretty. Everyone at JMU loves it here, and you can tell. There are **lots of smiling people here, and I like that**. That may sound really cheesy, but it's true. JMU is so awesome."

The College Prowler Take On...
Overall Experience

Students note that Harrisonburg comes up short, as far as bars and nightclubs go. As a result, apartments and houses have become the main party venues. Some students complain about the fact that most of JMU's students are heavily involved in the party scene. On Monday morning, as you dodge empty kegs and red plastic cups on your walk from the apartments to campus, it's hard to believe that not everyone takes part in the weekly hullabaloo. However, if you choose to abstain, even the most dedicated of drinkers will most likely respect your choice.

Although students will lodge some minor complaints about the excessively flourishing festivities, the whimsical weather, the perpetual parking pitfalls, and the lack of notable nightlife, the overall consensus is that JMU is a lovely location to live. With JMU's beautifully landscaped campus, the close proximity of the luscious Shenandoah Valley, the knowledgeable professors, friendly staff, and warm-hearted student body, it's not a huge surprise that students spend four or more very happy years at James Madison University. Freshmen, upperclassmen, graduates, and transfers agree that James Madison is a unique place to receive an education. The amiable attitude around town and campus has created a truly welcoming environment at James Madison University and helped Harrisonburg live up to its nickname, "the Friendly City."

The Inside Scoop

The Lowdown On...
The Inside Scoop

JMU Slang:

Know the slang, know the school. The following is a list of things you really need to know before coming to JMU. The more of these words you know, the better off you'll be.

The Airport Lounge (APL) – The students' name for the fourth floor of Warren Hall officially titled the "Loft," because it looks, well, like an airport lounge.

Baseball Lot – The parking lot up by the Modular Buildings and the baseball field.

Beast – Milwaukee's Best, a cheap beer that shows up at plenty of parties.

Breezer – Someone who works for the *Breeze*, JMU's student newspaper.

The Bridge – The name says it all; it's the overpass connecting main campus with the ISAT building, College Center, and Skyline Area.

The Commons – The area right outside D–Hall used for a variety of programs and advertisements, and also the place to meet your friends for lunch.

→

→

CRU – Not the rowing team, but the Christian organization Campus Crusade for Christ.

D-Hall – Students' fond nickname for the all-you-can-eat Gibbons Dining Hall.

E-campus – The secure online site where students register for classes, print unofficial transcripts, and other tasks of the academic official sort.

Frog – These are the only ones you'll meet that don't ribbit; they're your Freshman Orientation Guides. FYI: just in case you wanted to know, First Year Involvement, in Huffman Hall, is the hotspot for first-year students to chill and receive some academic assistance.

Go for the Gold – A set of Web-based sections designed by the Carrier Library staff to introduce students to the services and collections in Carrier Library. Translation: very boring, but very required for graduation.

Gravel Lot – The gravel parking lot on Grace Street.

ISAT – Integrated Science and Technology.

JAC – If you want to eat, go to the gym, access your records or survive on campus, you'll need to have your JAC card. If you hear students referring to their cards like old friends, it's because they're just that important.

Joe Info – Joe is a student's friend because it is an online database containing info on organizations, departments, clubs, individuals and other JMU related topics.

Kline's – The spot for the hottest ice cream in town.

Natty – Slang for Natural Light, one of the cheapest and most often consumed beers around.

The Pub – The nickname for Alston's Pub (pronounced Ahl–stun's).

Randoms – All the people you don't know who will walk into your parties.

SMAD – School of Media Art and Design

Trashby – Nickname for Ashby Crossing. It tends to look a wee bit trashy because, well, it is, thanks to the frequent partying.

Throwing Disc – Playing Frisbee.

"The" University of Virginia – A slogan at JMU stressing how much cooler we are than University of Virginia, located about an hour away in Charlottesville; this slogan also shows a little of the healthy rivalry that exists between the two schools.

The Village – One of the largest communities of residence halls on campus, not where the natives live.

Things I Wish I Knew Before Coming to JMU

- Transfer students are not guaranteed housing on campus.
- Harrisonburg is not a pedestrian-friendly town, especially if you live off campus.
- JMU is a pretty big party school.
- General education classes are more difficult than they seem; GSCI 101 is one of the worst.
- Online tests are harder than in-class tests.
- Don't park in the gravel lot if the weatherman is predicting rain, because when it rains, the gravel lot floods first.
- Some majors, like SMAD and SCOM are very competitive and hard to get into.
- Art, and all affiliated classes, is a closed major.
- Student assessment day in February sucks for everybody who has 45 to 70 credits to their name.
- JMU doesn't give too many holidays off; for example, be prepared to go to class on Labor Day and Presidents' Day.
- Don't take your winter coats and sweaters home during spring break because you might still need them afterwards!
- Parking briefly in a spot labeled "motorcycle parking" does not constitute parking legally; you will get a ticket.
- Putting your flashers on in front of Dukes does not constitute parking legally; you will get a ticket.
- Parking at 4 p.m. in a lot that opens to commuters at 4:30 p.m. is also illegal; you will get a ticket.
- Owning a vehicle with four wheels and parking it somewhere does not constitute parking legally; you will get a ticket.

Tips to Succeed at JMU

- Allow at least half an hour before class to find a parking spot.
- Get to know your professors.
- Be involved on campus in clubs and organizations.
- Do your homework.
- Always dispute test questions and bad grades.
- Get involved in dorm life; if possible, spend two years on campus.
- Know how to use Microsoft PowerPoint, Word, and Excel.
- See movies when they come to Grafton—it'll save you a few bucks each time.
- Check your e-mail, Blackboard, and the JMU Web site at least once a day.
- Go camping and hiking at least once before you graduate.
- Keep in touch with the parental units.
- Don't give in to caffeine and an all-nighter; get enough sleep the night before a final or midterm.
- Wear shower flip-flops. Seriously, just do it.
- Take a public speaking class. It will pay off by the time you've completed your umpteenth group presentation.
- Brush elbows with the townies; they are wonderful, friendly people.
- Go to class.
- Read the *Breeze*.

JMU Urban Legends

- While President Carrier was in office, the water ran out on Greek Row, and several of the brothers trekked over to the Carriers' house to take showers.
- For a case of the heebie-jeebies, students take a midnight peak at the Wilson Clock Tower. Rumor has it, if you stand on the Quad and the lighting is perfect, you might just see the shadow of the tower's resident ghost.
- More than 20 years ago, Eagle Hall experienced its share of bloodshed when two girls, "the Axe Murderesses of Eagle," took the lives of some number of residents. The rumor has been skewed so many times that no one actually remembers how many students were killed; numbers range anywhere from one to five.
- Newman Lake has been drained at least once by the police for reasons unknown. Legend has it that they were looking for a girl's body. Some even believe that her body was never found and that her ghost haunts the spot.

School Spirit

Plenty of us boast T-shirts reading, "I Bleed Purple," "JMU Dukes," or "Madison." These paraphernalia signify that, although our football team may not always win and our status will never be akin to that of Yale or Harvard, we are proud to be Madison students. Walking on campus, you can feel that students are proud to be one of nearly 15,000 who call JMU home. Turnout at football games, regardless of the scores, is impressive; clubs and organizations are added to the roster every year, in addition to countless more intramural teams. Students come to mingle and to socialize. Madison is a friendly school where students are involved in their campus and community. Whether it is politically, musically, journalistically, athletically, or socially, the bottom line is that JMU kids want to be associated with their University. Each year, competition for admission to James Madison University becomes more intense and more competitive because the school radiates a positive energy that is hard to ignore.

Traditions

For the Technology Junkies

In 2000, JMU hired Karim Altaii, an ISAT professor who decided it was time JMU had its own hovercraft. Two years later, the 550-pound Fenix, the brainchild of ten integrated science, technology, and computer science students, took flight one foot above the ground. The project took place in the ISAT/CS loading area, and the hovercraft can still be viewed today.

The Foxhills Block Party

Anybody who's anybody, anybody who wants to meet everybody, and anybody who wants to get smashed with everybody will be at the block party in Foxhills early in the school year. Usually, it takes place some time within the first month. The structure is typical—girls, guys, more girls, and beer—except that this party is a block long, from one end of the street to the other. To find it, just open your window; you'll hear the festivities from a mile away. Cops hear it too, and try to tighten the reins more every year.

Godwin Field Festival

On Saturday during Homecoming Week, the Godwin Field Festival gets the Dukes all riled up for live entertainment, games, and food. The whole shindig is aimed at pumping students up to watch the JMU football game that follows the Festival.

Greek Week

April showers bring May flowers and Greek Week, too. During Greek Week, sororities and fraternities participate in a week-long train of events, including Greek Letter and Greek T-Shirt Days, activities like tug-o-war and kickball, a barbeque, a Mr. and Ms. Greek Coronation, and Greek Sing. Greek Sing takes place annually, and includes a mix of song and dance to support a local or national charity.

Homecoming Week

During late October, Duke spirit abounds for a week of activities on campus. Events include a talent show, parade, football game, a night of entertainment (this year featured alumnist Phil Vassar), Sunset on the Quad, and the Godwin Field Festival.

James Madison Week

Madison Week hosts a variety of events to bring attention to the JMU campus. Throughout the week, students and visitors can witness the Wreath Laying at the James Madison Statue in front of Varner Hall, attend sessions, listen to speakers and satirical comedians, or watch the Battle for the Madison Cup, a commemorative debate, and a citizens' forum. For more information on Madison Week, visit *www.jmu.edu/birthday.*

JMU Holidayfest

Early each December, students and faculty have the chance to burrow into the Christmas spirit early on. The Holidayfest includes a concert in which seasonal music is performed by the JMU chorale, symphony orchestra, and brass band. Preceding the concert, audience members are invited to sing carols, enjoy hot chocolate and cookies, and witness the lighting of the JMU holiday tree on the campus Quadrangle in front of Wilson Hall.

The Kissing Rock

In the Normal School days (before JMU was coed), girls would entice their dates to smooch them on the Kissing Rock; it was believed her stone-standing pecking partner would someday be her husband. One might as well give it a try. The Kissing Rock is still located in the middle of the front of the Quad.

MACRoCk

It all started early in 1997, when the first Mid-Atlantic College Radio Conference was put on by WXJM, which is the JMU student-run radio station. Now, it's an annual tradition that brings punk, emo, and hardcore fans from up and down the East Coast. MACRoCk showcases DJs and managers from East Coast college radio stations, roundtable discussions, a label exposition, and many different concerts held in the Harrisonburg area over the course of a weekend. Thousands of music aficionados flock to JMU in the springtime in the name of student-run radio, independent music, independent thought, and independent business.

The Must-Dos

Many students believe their stay at JMU would not be complete without four interesting endeavors: streaking the Quad, traversing the tunnels under the Quad, hiking up into the cupola (the Wilson Clock Tower), and swimming in Newman Lake (the lake with the fountain, located by the main entrance to campus).

Parents' Weekend

Invite the parental units up for a couple days in mid-October for a little taste of life at Madison. Parents are invited to attend a variety of events, some of which have included: a Dukes' football game, a 5k Breast Cancer Walk/Run, a Beatles Tribute Show in Wilson Auditorium, and a concert by the JMU School of Music in the Convocation Center. In addition, the campus never looks finer than during Parents' Weekend; it is the only time of year you will ever see fresh bark chips spread, new flowers planted, tents erected, and cloth napkins and tablecloths displayed in D-Hall.

Sunset on the Quad

Every year during Homecoming, students gather on the Quad to gorge themselves on complimentary hot dogs and soda, watch the sunset and listen to the University's a cappella choirs and other entertainment groups perform.

Finding a Job or Internship

The Lowdown On... Finding a Job or Internship

JMU offers plenty of internship opportunities for students who are motivated enough to seek them out. Clubs and organizations on campus, like AWC (American Women in Communication) will host resumé seminars, internship workshops, or job fairs. Stay alert for valuable opportunities, learn more about local and national opportunities, begin forming relationships, and start getting in the know.

Advice

At JMU, not every major requires that you take an internship, but in almost every case, it is beneficial if you do. Find out early whether or not your major requires you to get some workforce experience. Stay ahead of the game, foster connections, stick your foot firmly in the door, and don't be afraid to put yourself out there. Also, keep your eye on whether or not internships you are interested in offer class credits or a salary; credits are the most common. If your major requires you to take an internship, make sure that you will get credit for your undertakings.

Career Center Resources & Services

- International internships (*www.jmu.edu/international*)
- JMU Academic Advising & Career Development (AACD)
- Career counseling
- AACD Resource Center
- MadisonTRAK
- Graduate school guides and advisors
- Freshman advising
- Hotlinks – *web.jmu.edu/career/web/Student/Links*

Firms That Most Frequently Hire Grads

CGI-AMS, Deloitte & Touche, Accenture, NVR/Ryan Homes, Locklead Martin, U.S. Government

Average Salary Information

The following statistics represent average starting salaries for JMU graduates by major. If the information for a specific major is not listed, it means that fewer than three students reported salary offers.

College of Business

• Average salary	$40,322
• Accounting	$40,840
• Computer Information Systems	$46,270
• Economics	$39,211
• Finance	$40,875
• Hospitality/Tourism Management	$30,643
• International Business	$35,000
• Management	$31,722
• Marketing	$35,872
• Quantitative Finance	$48,750

College of Integrated Science and Technology

• Average salary	$36,700
• Computer Science	$44,385
• Geographic Science	$31,600
• Health Science	$34,084
• Integrated Science and Technology	$42,462
• Kinesiology	$34,414
• Nursing	$36,507
• Psychology	$28,912
• Social Work	$23,429

College of Science and Mathematics

• Average salary	$29,570
• Biology	$26,691
• Mathematics	$36,477

College of Arts and Letters

- Average salary $28,482
- Anthropology $26,320
- Art $26,909
- English $25,330
- History $27,750
- International Affairs $33,665
- Media Arts and Design $25,863
- Modern Foreign Language $31,059
- Music $30,883
- Political Science $28,880
- Public Administration $31,563
- Social Science $31,413
- Sociology $31,902
- Speech Communication $26,293
- Technical and Scientific Communication $34,250

Alumni

The Lowdown On... Alumni

Web Site:

www.alumniconnections.com/olc/pub/JMD

Office:

JMU Office of Alumni Relations
2002 Alumni Drive
MSC 4402
Harrisonburg, Va 22807

(540) 568-6234;
(888) JMU-ALUM

Fax: (540) 568-3494

Hours of Operation:
Monday–Friday 8 a.m.–5 p.m.

Services Available:

Free, permanent, monthly e-mail summary of campus news, Alumni Association events and activities and JMU sports updates in addition to membership to regional alumni chapters and clubs.

Alumni Publications:

Montpelier, a quarterly publication for alumni, parents of JMU students, donors, faculty and staff members, and friends of the University.

Major Alumni Events

Reunion Weekend and Homecoming are the biggest events for JMU alumni. Homecoming takes place in late October, and Reunion Weekend in late April. In between, there are luncheons, meetings, happy hours, and countless invitations to athletic events to keep alumni as involved or uninvolved as they would like to be. There are also plenty of athletic events specifically for alumni, such as the Richmond Alumni Golf Tournament and the Metro Dukes Alumni Golf Tournament at Virginia Oaks in June and the Strawberry Hill horse races in April. Alumni also have the opportunity to travel with the AHI Corporation, better known as Alumni Holidays.

Did You Know?

Dr. Marcia Angell (Class of '60) – Senior lecturer in the Department of Social Medicine at Harvard Medical School and former executive editor, *New England Journal of Medicine.*

David Gill (Class of '76) – Successful and well-respected artist.

Robert "Phoef " Sutton (Class of '81) – The writer and producer of TV show *Cheers.*

Phil Vassar (Class of '85) – Award-winning country music writer/performer. He was the recipient of the 2002 Academy of Country Music's "Top New Male Artist."

Charles Haley (Class of '87) – The only player in NFL history to own five Super Bowl rings.

Delvin Joyce (Class of '00) – A punt returner who signed as a free agent with the New York Giants in February 2002.

Curtis Keaton (Class of '00) – Now a reserve running back with the New Orleans Saints, he was originally drafted by the Cincinnati Bengals in the fourth round of the 2000 NFL Draft.

Also, with 41 alumni serving as Peace Corp volunteers in developing countries, JMU was ranked fifth nationally in 2003 among medium-size colleges whose alumni serve abroad.

Student Organizations

African Student Organization
Asian Students
Baha'i Association
Best Buddies
Blues Tones
Brothers of New Direction
Campus Crusade for Christ
Canterbury Episcopal Campus Ministry
Catholic Campus Ministry
Contemporary Gospel
Devoted
EARTH
EQUAL
Exit 245
Fashion Design Club
Flute Club
French Club
Gardy Loo
Geology Club
Habitat for Humanity
Harmony
Honor Council
Honors Publication
IEEE Computer Society
Inspirational Ensemble Club
International Justice Mission
International Student
International Trumpet Guild
Into Hymn
Italian Cultural Society
JMU Dance Theatre
JMU Four-Square
JMU Freethinkers
JMU Horn Club
Keyboard Association
Kickball Club
Latino Student Alliance

LDSSA
Links
Low Key
Lutheran Campus Ministry
MANGA
Madison Bugle Corps
Madison Dance Club
MGDA
Madison Historians
Madison International Association
Madison Investment Fund
Madison Marketing Association
Madison Motorcycle Club
Madison Motor Sports
Madison Project
Madison Society
Martial Arts Club
Mathematics and Statistics Club
Middle Eastern Club
Mortar Board
Mountain Biking Club
Muslim Student Association
National Residence Hall Honorary
National Society of Collegiate Scholars
National Society of Minorities in Hospitality
Note-oriety
One in Four
Operation Smile
Optimist Club
Outing Club
Student Speech/Language/Hearing Association
Physician Assistant Student Society (PASS)
Pre-Occupational Therapy Society
Pre-Pharmacy Society
Pre-Physical Therapy Society
Presbyterian Campus Ministry
PROMotion
Psychology Club
Roller Hockey Club
Roop Group: Past and Present
Rotaract Club
Sailing Club
Science Fiction Fantasy Guild
Semper Fidelis Society
Sign Language Club
Skyline Winterguard
Society of Manufacturing Engineers
Society of Physics Students
Sociology Club
Spanish Club
Sports Club Council
Stratford Players
Student Ambassadors
Student Athletic Training Association
Student Duke Club
Student Education
Student Government Association
Student Officials Association
Students for Camp Heartland

Students for Minority Outreach
Swing Dance Club
Tae Kwon Do Club
Trombone Association
University Graphics
University Program Board
Unix Users Group
Up 'Til Dawn
Virginia Biotechnology Association
Wesley Foundation
Women of Color
WXJM-FM
Young Life Leadership

The Best & Worst

The Ten **BEST** Things About JMU

1. The Quad
2. The Arboretum
3. Festival's chicken and mashed potato dinners
4. Movies at Grafton
5. Theme parties
6. Half-off Wednesdays at IHOP
7. The JMU Marching Band
8. *The Breeze*, JMU's student newspaper
9. The friendly atmosphere
10. Plenty of classes cancelled for inclement weather

The Ten WORST Things About JMU

1. Saturday make-up days for inclement weather
2. Winter weather in the springtime
3. The guy/girl ratio
4. Lack of bars and nightclubs
5. The Modular Building
6. The parking quandary
7. Lack of diversity on campus
8. The long hike from ISAT to the Quad
9. No double-punching on weekends
10. Community showers

Visiting

The Lowdown On...
Visiting

Hotel Information:

Belle Meade Red Carpet Inn
3210 S Main St.
Harrisonburg, VA 22801
(540) 434-6704
(800) 251-1962
Distance from Campus: 2.8 miles
Price: $50

Best Western
45 Burgess Rd.
Harrisonburg, VA 22801
(540) 433-6089
(800) 21-Guest
Distance from Campus: 1.4 miles
Price: $70

Comfort Inn Harrisonburg
1440 E Market Street
Harrisonburg, VA 22801
(540) 433-6066
(800) 228-5150
Distance from Campus: 1.3 miles
Price: $90

➜

Days Inn
1131 Forest Hill Rd.
Harrisonburg, VA 22801
(540) 433-9353
(800) Days-Inn
Distance from Campus:
0.8 miles
Price: $52

Econo Lodge Harrisonburg
1703 E Market St.
Harrisonburg, VA 22801
(540) 433-2576
(800) 553-2666
Distance from Campus:
1.7 miles
Price: $65

Hampton Inn
85 University Blvd.
Harrisonburg, VA 22801
(540) 432-1111
(800) Hamp-ton
Distance from Campus:
1.6 miles
Price: $75

Holiday Inn
1400 East Market St.
Harrisonburg, VA 22801
(540) 433-2521
(800) 703-7037
Distance from Campus:
1.2 miles
Price: $109

Holiday Inn Express Harrisonburg
3325 S Main St.
Harrisonburg, VA 22801
(540) 433-9999
(800) Holi-day
Distance from Campus:
2.9
Price: $76

Jameson Inn
1881 Evelyn Byrd Ave.
Harrisonburg, VA 22801
(540) 442-1515
(800) 822-5252
Distance from Campus:
1.7 miles
Price: $73

Joshua Wilton House
412 S Main St.
Harrisonburg, VA 22801
(540) 434-4464
(800) 2Wil-ton
Distance from Campus:
0.3 miles
Price: $77

Marriott Courtyard
1890 Evelyn Byrd Ave.
Harrisonburg, VA 22801
(540) 432-3031
(888) 236-2427
Distance from Campus:
1.7 miles
Price: $90

Ramada Inn South
1 Pleasant Valley Rd.
Harrisonburg, VA 22801
(540) 434-9981
Distance from Campus:
3 miles
Price: $52

Sleep Inn
1891 Evelyn Byrd Ave.
Harrisonburg, VA 22801
(540) 433-7100
(800) 424-6423
Distance from Campus:
1.7 miles
Price: $110

Stonewall Jackson Inn, B&B
547 E Market St.
Harrisonburg, VA 22801
(540) 433-8233
(800) 445-5330
Distance from Campus:
1.5 miles
Price: $99–$150

Super 8 Motel - Harrisonburg
3330 S Main St.
Harrisonburg, VA 22801
Distance from Campus:
2.9 miles
Price: $65

The Village Inn
4979 S Valley Pike
Harrisonburg, VA 22801
(540) 434-7355
(800) 736-7355
Distance from Campus:
0.7 miles
Price: $60

Take a Campus Virtual Tour

www.jmu.edu/admissions/visit

To Schedule a Group Information Session or Interview

During the fall and winter, the Office of Admissions offers group information sessions and student-guided tours Monday through Friday and, occasionally, on Saturdays. In July, the same schedule applies. In August, informational sessions are available along with a booklet to help you take a self-guided tour. For more information or to view the current visitation schedule, check out *www.jmu.edu/admissions/visit*. Questions and comments? Call the Campus Visitation Center, which can be reached at (540) 568-5681 or e-mail visit-jmu@jmu.edu. The Office of Admissions is open Monday through Friday from 8 a.m. to 5 p.m.

If you were psyched for an interview, you may want to de-psych, because JMU does not offer them. In place of an interview, JMU requires a personal statement in the application. It's a sort of interview on paper.

Campus Tours

Tours of the Charles River campus depart from the Admissions Reception Center. Contact Admissions at least two weeks prior to your visit, as visitation schedules are prone to change. The easiest way to schedule a visit is to fill out a reservation form electronically at *www.jmu.edu/admissions/visit/reservation.shtml*. Once you have submitted the form, you will receive automatic electronic confirmation that will include directions and local lodging information. However, if you are bringing a group of eight or more people, please contact the visitation center at (540) 568-5681.

Overnight Visits

Not available; a freshman parents' weekend was held several years ago, but with a very poor turnout. However, Parent's Weekend is a huge deal at JMU, even if mommy and daddy stay in a hotel.

Directions to Campus

Driving from the North

- To reach campus from the north on I-81, take exit 247 for US 33 West.
- Turn left at the first traffic signal onto Cantrell Ave.
- Pass two traffic signals on Cantrell Ave.
- After the crest of a hill, turn left at the third Cantrell traffic signal at Rockingham Hospital onto Mason St.
- Turn left at the next stop sign.

Driving from the South

- From the south, take I-81.
- Take Exit 245 and at the top of the ramp turn left onto Port Republic Rd.
- Take a right at the second light onto JMU's campus.

Driving from the West

- From the east, take I-64 East.
- Exit onto I-81 North.
- Get off on Exit 245.
- Take a left at the stop light at the top of the ramp onto Port Republic Rd.
- Take a right at the second light onto JMU's campus.

Driving from the East

- From the west, take I-64 West.
- Exit onto I-81 North.
- Get off on Exit 245
- Take a left at the stop light at the top of the ramp onto Port Republic Rd.
- Take a right at the second light onto JMU's campus.

Words to Know

Academic Probation – A suspension imposed on a student if he or she fails to keep up with the school's minimum academic requirements. Those unable to improve their grades after receiving this warning can face dismissal.

Beer Pong/Beirut – A drinking game involving cups of beer arranged in a pyramid shape on each side of a table. The goal is to get a ping pong ball into one of the opponent's cups by throwing the ball or hitting it with a paddle. If the ball lands in a cup, the opponent is required to drink the beer.

Bid – An invitation from a fraternity or sorority to 'pledge' (join) that specific house.

Blue-Light Phone – Brightly-colored phone posts with a blue light bulb on top. These phones exist for security purposes and are located at various outside locations around most campuses. In an emergency, a student can pick up one of these phones (free of charge) to connect with campus police or a security escort.

Campus Police – Police who are specifically assigned to a given institution. Campus police are typically not regular city officers; they are employed by the university in a full-time capacity.

Club Sports – A level of sports that falls somewhere between varsity and intramural. If a student is unable to commit to a varsity team but has a lot of passion for athletics, a club sport could be a better, less intense option. Even less demanding, intramural (IM) sports often involve no traveling and considerably less time.

Cocaine – An illegal drug. Also known as "coke" or "blow," cocaine often resembles a white crystalline or powdery substance. It is highly addictive and dangerous.

Common Application – An application with which students can apply to multiple schools.

Course Registration – The period of official class selection for the upcoming quarter or semester. Prior to registration, it is best to prepare several back-up courses in case a particular class becomes full. If a course is full, students can place themselves on the waitlist, although this still does not guarantee entry.

Division Athletics – Athletic classifications range from Division I to Division III. Division IA is the most competitive, while Division III is considered to be the least competitive.

Dorm – A dorm (or dormitory) is an on-campus housing facility. Dorms can provide a range of options from suite-style rooms to more communal options that include shared bathrooms. Most first-year students live in dorms. Some upperclassmen who wish to stay on campus also choose this option.

Early Action – An application option with which a student can apply to a school and receive an early acceptance response without a binding commitment. This system is becoming less and less available.

Early Decision – An application option that students should use only if they are certain they plan to attend the school in question. If a student applies using the early decision option and is admitted, he or she is required and bound to attend that university. Admission rates are usually higher among students who apply through early decision, as the student is clearly indicating that the school is his or her first choice.

Ecstasy – An illegal drug. Also known as "E" or "X," ecstasy looks like a pill and most resembles an aspirin. Considered a party drug, ecstasy is very dangerous and can be deadly.

Ethernet – An extremely fast Internet connection available in most university-owned residence halls. To use an Ethernet connection properly, a student will need a network card and cable for his or her computer.

Fake ID – A counterfeit identification card that contains false information. Most commonly, students get fake IDs with altered birthdates so that they appear to be older than 21 (and therefore of legal drinking age). Even though it is illegal, many college students have fake IDs in hopes of purchasing alcohol or getting into bars.

Frosh – Slang for "freshman" or "freshmen."

Hazing – Initiation rituals administered by some fraternities or sororities as part of the pledging process. Many universities have outlawed hazing due to its degrading, and sometimes dangerous, nature.

Intramurals (IMs) – A popular, and usually free, sport league in which students create teams and compete against one another. These sports vary in competitiveness and can include a range of activities—everything from billiards to water polo. IM sports are a great way to meet people with similar interests.

Keg – Officially called a half-barrel, a keg contains roughly 200 12-ounce servings of beer.

LSD – An illegal drug, also known as acid, this hallucinogenic drug most commonly resembles a tab of paper.

Marijuana – An illegal drug, also known as weed or pot; along with alcohol, marijuana is one of the most commonly-found drugs on campuses across the country.

Major –The focal point of a student's college studies; a specific topic that is studied for a degree. Examples of majors include physics, English, history, computer science, economics, business, and music. Many students decide on a specific major before arriving on campus, while others are simply "undecided" until declaring a major. Those who are extremely interested in two areas can also choose to double major.

Meal Block – The equivalent of one meal. Students on a meal plan usually receive a fixed number of meals per week. Each meal, or "block," can be redeemed at the school's dining facilities in place of cash. Often, a student's weekly allotment of meal blocks will be forfeited if not used.

Minor – An additional focal point in a student's education. Often serving as a complement or addition to a student's main area of focus, a minor has fewer requirements and prerequisites to fulfill than a major. Minors are not required for graduation from most schools; however some students who want to explore many different interests choose to pursue both a major and a minor.

Mushrooms – An illegal drug. Also known as "'shrooms," this drug resembles regular mushrooms but is extremely hallucinogenic.

Off-Campus Housing – Housing from a particular landlord or rental group that is not affiliated with the university. Depending on the college, off-campus housing can range from extremely popular to non-existent. Students who choose to live off campus are typically given more freedom, but they also have to deal with possible subletting scenarios, furniture, bills, and other issues. In addition to these factors, rental prices and distance often affect a student's decision to move off campus.

Office Hours – Time that teachers set aside for students who have questions about coursework. Office hours are a good forum for students to go over any problems and to show interest in the subject material.

Pledging – The early phase of joining a fraternity or sorority, pledging takes place after a student has gone through rush and received a bid. Pledging usually lasts between one and two semesters. Once the pledging period is complete and a particular student has done everything that is required to become a member, that student is considered a brother or sister. If a fraternity or a sorority would decide to "haze" a group of students, this initiation would take place during the pledging period.

Private Institution – A school that does not use tax revenue to subsidize education costs. Private schools typically cost more than public schools and are usually smaller.

Prof – Slang for "professor."

Public Institution – A school that uses tax revenue to subsidize education costs. Public schools are often a good value for in-state residents and tend to be larger than most private colleges.

Quarter System (or Trimester System) – A type of academic calendar system. In this setup, students take classes for three academic periods. The first quarter usually starts in late September or early October and concludes right before Christmas. The second quarter usually starts around early to mid–January and finishes up around March or April. The last academic quarter, or "third quarter," usually starts in late March or early April and finishes up in late May or Mid-June. The fourth quarter is summer. The major difference between the quarter system and semester system is that students take more, less comprehensive courses under the quarter calendar.

RA (Resident Assistant) – A student leader who is assigned to a particular floor in a dormitory in order to help to the other students who live there. An RA's duties include ensuring student safety and providing assistance wherever possible.

Recitation – An extension of a specific course; a review session. Some classes, particularly large lectures, are supplemented with mandatory recitation sessions that provide a relatively personal class setting.

Rolling Admissions – A form of admissions. Most commonly found at public institutions, schools with this type of policy continue to accept students throughout the year until their class sizes are met. For example, some schools begin accepting students as early as December and will continue to do so until April or May.

Room and Board – This figure is typically the combined cost of a university-owned room and a meal plan.

Room Draw/Housing Lottery – A common way to pick on-campus room assignments for the following year. If a student decides to remain in university-owned housing, he or she is assigned a unique number that, along with seniority, is used to determine his or her housing for the next year.

Rush – The period in which students can meet the brothers and sisters of a particular chapter and find out if a given fraternity or sorority is right for them. Rushing a fraternity or a sorority is not a requirement at any school. The goal of rush is to give students who are serious about pledging a feel for what to expect.

Semester System – The most common type of academic calendar system at college campuses. This setup typically includes two semesters in a given school year. The fall semester starts around the end of August or early September and concludes before winter vacation. The spring semester usually starts in mid-January and ends in late April or May.

Student Center/Rec Center/Student Union – A common area on campus that often contains study areas, recreation facilities, and eateries. This building is often a good place to meet up with fellow students; depending on the school, the student center can have a huge role or a non-existent role in campus life.

Student ID – A university-issued photo ID that serves as a student's key to school-related functions. Some schools require students to show these cards in order to get into dorms, libraries, cafeterias, and other facilities. In addition to storing meal plan information, in some cases, a student ID can actually work as a debit card and allow students to purchase things from bookstores or local shops.

Suite – A type of dorm room. Unlike dorms that feature communal bathrooms shared by the entire floor, suites offer bathrooms shared only among the suite. Suite-style dorm rooms can house anywhere from two to ten students.

TA (Teacher's Assistant) – An undergraduate or grad student who helps in some manner with a specific course. In some cases, a TA will teach a class, assist a professor, grade assignments, or conduct office hours.

Undergraduate – A student in the process of studying for his or her bachelor's degree.

ABOUT THE AUTHOR

Now that my cursor is finally reaching the bottom of this document, I'm relieved and excited. I feel satisfied with the research and the (excessive amounts of) time I spent on this guidebook's creation. It was a great opportunity to use my creativity and writing skills to help out wandering high school seniors and their parents, all searching for the school of their choice. I'm now a senior at James Madison University, relentlessly pursuing a career in print journalism, working as the assistant Variety/Focus editor at the *Breeze* (the school paper), and firefighting in the summers in Oregon. Just as I couldn't have told you my freshman year I'd be in Virginia a couple years later, I can't tell you where in the world I'll be after graduation. However, I feel confident that wherever I end up, my life has been enriched by living in Harrisonburg and attending JMU. Whether or not you decide to join the Madison ranks, I hope this guidebook has helped you out, answered some of your questions, and perhaps even entertained you.

With the knowledge that I haven't won an Oscar or a Pulitzer yet, I still have a list of people I would love to recognize. Thank you, God, first of all, for this opportunity; thank you, Mom and Dad, for bugging me about this book and for always believing in and supporting me with your love, encouragement, and humor; Kyle, my favorite lil' big bro; Susan, the Machine, for being my intellectual twin and my soul sister; all of my awesome friends at IUP and SOU, for making my freshman and sophomore years unbeatable; Kelly, Natalie, Kate, Corey, Nini, and all my L-Town homies, for being the amazing friends that you are; my roommates Kim, Brook, and Chris, for putting up with me and my silly questions; my roomies for next year Carly, Kelsey, Kemper, Diana, and Katie, for all their love and prayers; all my JMU friends who are too numerous too name, but too precious to leave out; and all the people at College Prowler, especially, for their patience and flexibility. Thank you!

Sylva Florence, Author
sylvaflorence@collegeprowler.com

Schools of the South

Headin' down south? This book will help you find your way to the perfect school!

Schools of the South
7¼" X 10", 773 Pages Paperback
$29.95 Retail
1-59658-503-X

Southern pride is always strong. Whether it's across town or across state, many Southern students are devoted to their home sweet home. *Schools of the South* offers an honest student perspective on 36 universities available south of the Mason-Dixon.

Untangling the Ivy League

The ultimate book for everything Ivy!

UNTANGLING THE IVY LEAGUE
7¼" X 10", 567 Pages Paperback
$24.95 Retail
1-59658-500-5

Ivy League students, alumni, admissions officers, and other top insiders get together to tell it like it is. *Untangling the Ivy League* covers every aspect—from admissions and athletics to secret societies and urban legends—of the nation's eight oldest, wealthiest, and most competitive colleges and universities.

Pros and Cons

Still can't figure out if this is the right school for you? You've already read through this in-depth guide; why not list the pros and cons? It will really help with narrowing down your decision and determining whether or not this school is right for you.

Pros	Cons
....	....
....	....
....	....
....	....
....	....
....	....
....	....
....	....
....	....
....	....
....	....
....	....
....	....

Pros and Cons

Still can't figure out if this is the right school for you? You've already read through this in-depth guide; why not list the pros and cons? It will really help with narrowing down your decision and determining whether or not this school is right for you.

Pros	Cons

Notes

College Prowler®

Notes

Notes

COLLEGE PROWLER®

Notes

COLLEGE PROWLER®

Notes

COLLEGE PROWLER®

Notes

Notes

Notes

Notes

COLLEGE PROWLER®

Notes

College Prowler®

Notes

Notes